End

of the

Portage

Also by Phil Weir

Canoeing the Mountain: Gifts from the Waters

End
of the
Portage

A Canoe Memoir

Phil Weir

Wildwaters Publishing

Published in Canada by: Wildwaters Publishing
106 – 55 Blackberry Drive, New Westminster, BC
www.wildwaterspublishing.com

Front cover photo, back cover photo, and author photo by Phil Weir
Cover design by Phil Weir and by Jim Bisakowski: BookDesign.ca
Text design and typesetting by Jim Bisakowski: BookDesign.ca
Printed in the United States of America

Weir, Phil, 1951-, author
        End of the Portage / Phil Weir.

Issued in print and electronic formats.
ISBN 978-0-9920665-3-6 (pbk)
ISBN 978-0-9920665-4-3 (mobi)
ISBN 978-0-9920665-5-0 (epub)

1. Sports and Recreation – Canoes and Canoeing – Canada –
        Ontario --Petawawa River.
2. Camping – Canada – Ontario--Algonquin Park
3. Travel – Canada – Ontario
4. Travel – Special Interest – Adventure
5. Whitewater canoeing—Canada--Ontario.

For information on ordering, please see: www.wildwaterspublishing.com

To my love,
my best friend,
and my long-suffering editor,
Jill

and to
Jody, Daniel and Patrick

The Petawawa River begins with rain and snow in the Algonquin Park highlands of Eastern Ontario, drains eastward, and pours into the Ottawa River. Eventually these, and more combined waters, join with the Saint Laurence River and travel northeast, to become part of the Atlantic Ocean.

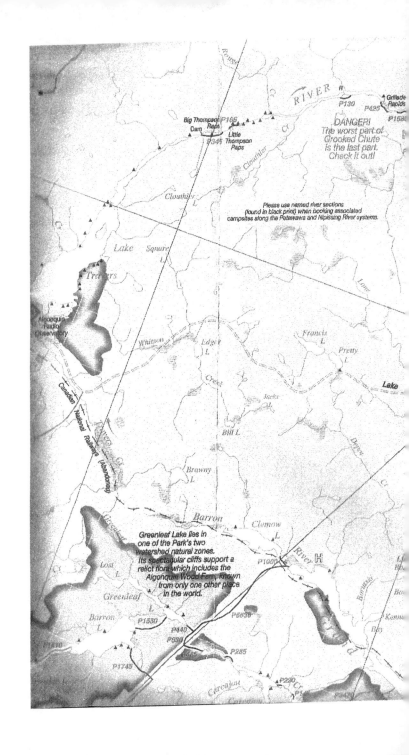

RIVER

P130   Grillade
                Rapids
    P425   P1580

Big Thompson P165
Dam   Rapids
        Little   **DANGER!**
P345   Thompson   The worst part of
        Paps   Crooked Chute
                         is the last part.
                         Check it out!

Clouthier

Clouthier
        L.

                    Please use named river sections
                (found in black print) when booking associated
            campsites along the Petawawa and Nipissing River systems.

Lake   Square
            L.

Travers   Lone

                            Francis
                               L.

Algonquin   Pretty
Radio   Whitson   Edger   L.
Observatory   L.
                                                        Lake

                    Creek

Canadian   Jacks
                              L.

National
        Railway (Abandoned)   Bill L.

                    Brawny
                       L.

                        Barron   Clemow

            Greenleaf Lake lies in   L.
            one of the Park's two
            watershed natural zones.   River   **H**
            Its spectacular cliffs support a
            relict flora which includes the   P1000
            Algonquin Wood Fern, known
    Lost   from only one other place
      L.   in the world.

    Greenleaf
                    L.

Barron   P1530
  L.   P440   P6650
                  P890
P1410   P285

    P1745

            Carcajou   P250

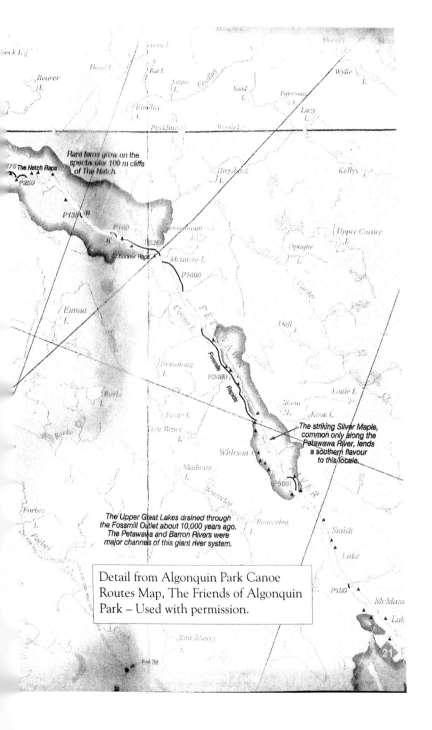

Rare ferns grow on the spectacular 100 m cliffs of The Natch.

The striking Silver Maple, common only along the Petawawa River, lends a southern flavour to this locale.

The Upper Great Lakes drained through the Fossmill Outlet about 10,000 years ago. The Petawawa and Barron Rivers were major channels of this giant river system.

Detail from Algonquin Park Canoe Routes Map, The Friends of Algonquin Park – Used with permission.

Before Starting

This story is true, from my point of view, as true as memories can be.

But this book should not be used as a guidebook or a trip planner. Don't rely on my words or your own luck to see you through. Luck can change quicker than the weather. Skill sets are different for each person. Distances and other factors may not be accurate and, due to many factors, the Petawawa River is a different river every day. The running of rapids is a risky activity, and neither the author nor the publishers can be responsible for errors in judgement leading to injuries or fatalities. For any adventure in the wild, a traveler should first do their own pre-trip homework, gain the needed skills, collect accurate up-to-date information, and plan carefully. Once on-site, they should scout whenever possible, make their own observations, weigh all the circumstances and adapt. Even so, there will surely be surprises. Stay positive.

- Phil Weir, Ottawa

Highly Recommended Resources:

- *PETAWAWA RIVER WHITEWATER GUIDE, Algonquin Provincial Park* By George Drought
- *Algonquin Park CANOE ROUTES Map* (most recent edition)

Both are published by, and available from, *The Friends of Algonquin Park*: http://www.algonquinpark.on.ca
613-637-2828 and from the Algonquin Park Visitor Centre Bookstore and Nature Shop, the Algonquin Park Logging Museum, the Algonquin Park West Gate, the East Gate, most Backcountry (Interior) Access Point Offices, and other retailers.

PART 1

Paddling alone in a canoe in remote wild places is something which, by choice or circumstances, most people never do. But I'm lucky. I've been fortunate to have had a lot of coaching and many wonderful paddling experiences over the years, so for me, when I climb in a canoe and let it take me away, it's almost like being on a magic carpet ride. I love gliding over water like a bird through the air, as nature passes by in every direction. My canoe, and what it enables me to do, gives me a deep feeling of connection with nature. Plus, without any companions along, a solo canoe trip usually turns into a long meditation.

There's work to do, but also many quiet hours on the water or wandering around camp, to savour moments that would probably be interrupted or unappreciated if others were there. A natural romanticism arises that's rare in this busy world. Extended opportunities for private thoughts turn my focus outward to the marvels of nature, and also inward to the quiet, sometimes loud, voices speaking inside.

Now and then all the tasks are done. There's time to just relax and watch patterns in the sky, listen to the wind, or simply let the mind drift. There's also time to pay attention to fleeting things, such as the perfect little eddies that twirl behind the paddle, and the way they sometimes make soft gurgling sounds as they spin away. I might lie on a calm evening, reclining on my PFD (personal flotation device, often inaccurately called a life jacket), idly watching smoke from the campfire drift ever so slowly, horizontally across the water. Subtle weather changes are noticed, as are little sounds in the forest. Time becomes less important than the amount of daylight. Positive sensations come easily. And all of this gets steadily better as the days and nights of a trip go by.

When I paddle solo through the natural world, there's no denying that a personal journey moves along inside of me too. Many hours are spent enjoying the wonders of nature, and solving problems related to the trip. But if I choose, the depth of introspection can become like a personal counselling session. Ideas and considerations pop up that have been neglected or postponed. There might be new directions of thought, sometimes seemingly out of the blue, or brought about by serendipitous events. I get increasingly philosophical. Metaphors seem to be everywhere, such as the way life's rocks make the waters part, then they flow back together.

At any moment, I might be casually observing the patterns of lines in a rock, or the shape of a tree. But just as easily, I could be sorting through a personal problem, even pondering who I am, where I am in my life, what I should do, or sorting out my feelings about something. Without any companions to affect my flow of thought, I keep only my own counsel, and my mind sometimes travels to places it might otherwise not go. This can happen during quiet times or when busily occupied; sometimes even in the midst of a frightening close call.

Nearly all my many canoe trips over the years have been with my wife Jill, my children, friends, or groups of high school students. My dearest memories are of the family outings, but each configuration of groups has its unique characteristics and merits. A solo trip isn't a replacement for any of these, just a special treat.

Jill understands, and accepts my need to head off alone with my boat now and then. She knows I'll return tired, but quite a bit less tense. I'll be more animated, refreshed, in a better mood, in better balance. And of course, I'll have stories to tell.

Solo trips leave me loving and appreciating my wife and kids more than ever, and also life in general. It's wonderful to go, and great to come back, richer for the time. Despite the surprises, challenges, and sometimes adversity that I've encountered out there, I believe I've always returned home a better person after every solo trip – even this one.

End of the Portage

2

In September, I would start my last year in the classroom. By the following summer I would have completed 30 years of teaching, and be retired. I wanted to do something special. Jill and I discussed it, and set aside a few days in the middle of August 2005 for me to head off alone.

In great spirits, I loaded the car, tied my fourteen-year-old red Mad River canoe on top, and set off to start a four-day, 50-kilometre solo paddle down the Petawawa River in Algonquin Park. Two days into that memorable trip I got sloppy on a long run of whitewater, and paid the price.

It's embarrassing to say, but this wasn't my first major canoeing accident. Fourteen years earlier, in 1991, while paddling the Mountain River in the Northwest Territories on a wilderness whitewater trip with friends, my friend Roger and I severely wrapped our rental canoe around a rock offshore in frigid, pounding, deep water. Fortunately, with a lot of effort and teamwork, our group was able to make that canoe rise again. We fixed it up into reasonably good shape and all of us floated on and successfully completed our wonderful journey.[1]

---

1 Weir, Phil. 2014. *Canoeing the Mountain: Gifts from the Water.*
Wildwaters Publishing. New Westminster, BC

My August 2005 wipeout on the Petawawa was by far my most serious accident since then. During the in-between years, I had paddled extensively, and my whitewater skills had grown much more polished. Also, as a high school teacher who for decades was very involved with Outdoor Education, I taught hundreds of teenagers and adults how to canoe. With other staff, I led dozens of high school canoe-camping trips, some of them including whitewater, and all of them emphasizing safety. But good group record or not, out there all alone, I wrecked my canoe.

It was in the early evening of my long second day out. After paddling 24 kilometres during two full days from the put-in on Lake Travers, I had arrived at Rollway Rapids. Rollway is a long, exciting stretch of rapids, an 800-metre whitewater paddlers dream. It's a natural slalom course, and requires almost constant zigging, zagging and rock-dodging. Always tricky to paddle, it's great fun for those with the skills.

Foolishly, I had been too lazy and too cocky to carry my gear even part way down the rapids using the convenient good portage trail. This meant I was attempting to paddle the big rapid's entire length with my canoe fully loaded. I believed I could manage this, and had done it before. But that was in higher water. This time my run didn't end as planned, and on a solo trip there's only one person you can blame.

Rollway is aptly named, an escalator of tumbling Class 3 and 4 whitewater that can easily roll a canoe. On the rating scale of a rapid's difficulty, it's at the upper limit for navigation in an open canoe, even one with front and rear floatation airbags like mine. The challenge is always to find a route friendly enough to float the boat through the abundant boulders, without tipping or smashing it. This requires fast steering manoeuvres, and clear thinking. I made it more than half way down.

Looking at the rapids from shore, an observer sees hundreds of what I like to call white horses popping up and down. These are the dancing splashes and plumes of spray that happen when fast-moving water slams into solid obstacles – mainly rocks. A paddler must always be realistic, and adapt to fit the conditions. I should have portaged my gear.

There's a little brass memorial cross, about two thirds of the way down the 820-metre portage trail located on river-right (the right-hand side when going down a river). I'd seen it before, on previous trips. Standing only about a foot tall (30 centimetres), it's a reminder of the fact that canoeist Blair Fraser died in these rapids in May of 1968. He was traveling with a group of friends who called themselves "The Voyageurs." The story I heard is that he and his group had no intention of running these rapids. But in the high waters of May, Fraser and his paddling partner somehow missed the take-out for the portage. His canoe was swept into Rollway and tragically, he wiped out and drowned. His partner made it to shore and survived. Later his friends came back and installed the little cross, partly as a memorial, and partly as a caution to other paddlers. It stands close to the river's edge, beside a place where one can look out over the water and easily see the clear signs of a hazardous drop over a long underwater ledge that crosses the whole river at that point.

Most people travelling the river choose to carry their boat and all their gear to the very end of the portage trail. Having bypassed the entire rapid, they put-in a short way after the last splashes. Some paddlers choose to portage only the gear to the end of the run, to lighten their boat and ensure that everything stays safe. Then they go back and ride their empty canoe all the way through the rapids. Still others also portage their gear down the trail the whole way, but only carry their boat two thirds of the way, to a small put-in spot located a few metres downriver from the cross. This choice gets them past the dangerous ledge, but they still get to have a wonderful rollercoaster ride through the final 300 metres, before they pull over and pick up their gear.

No matter which option a person or group chooses, or how experienced they might be, if they're thinking of possibly running even part of it, Rollway must always be scouted. Like most whitewater rivers, the Petawawa is to some extent a different river every day. Small changes in conditions can have dramatic effects. Besides variation in the weather, water levels can fluctuate, rocks appear or disappear, channels open or close, and currents strengthen, weaken, or change locations. Also, unexpected objects might have floated down the river, such as newly fallen trees, logs or other obstructions, and be waiting to block the path of a moving boat, causing serious problems.

I did of course pull my canoe out by the yellow Algonquin Park "Mister Canoehead" portage trailhead sign. Leaving it full of gear, pulled up on the bank, I walked along and scouted the run in detail to its very end and back up again. I decided it looked safe, given my experience and abilities.

Because the summer had been exceptionally dry, the river was lower than I'd ever seen it. On my first day out, I had almost decided to scrub the whole trip and go home after only a few hours, because when I reached Big Thompson, the first rapid, I was shocked to see such a small volume of water flowing through.

There was only one small channel with enough water to allow a navigable route. It was obvious my journey would involve a lot more bumping, banging, and probably more dragging, lining, and portaging than usual. But I really wanted to do the trip, and felt the need to accomplish something special.

Getting the opportunity to be out in the wild alone for a few days was so precious. Who knows when I would get the chance again? After weighing all the factors, I made my silent commitment, and carried all my gear to the end of the portage around Big Thompson. Then I walked back and successfully ran it in the empty canoe. It turned out to be easy; a lovely way to end that first day.

Day two I got up at dawn at the small campsite by the second rapid, Little Thompson. After breakfast I took down my little yellow solo tent, re-sorted my big turquoise canoe pack and blue food barrel, loaded the canoe, and pushed off. Most of the day had been a slow steady paddle, except for a couple of flatwater sections where I rested my paddle across the gunwales and lay back on the airbags, letting the canoe drift.

By the time I arrived at Rollway I'd gone through a few relatively gentle rapids. Although "boney" and technical, requiring some twists and turns, there had been no problem. Even the first part of Crooked Chute, before my mandatory take-out to portage past its big hairpin turn, was fairly basic, a lovely pleasure cruise. That old Mad River was a sturdy ABS Royalex "foam sandwich" plastic canoe. With the water so shallow and the current weak, it lightly bumped and grazed past a few rocks along the way, but slid by easily. She was a great, tough, whitewater boat. We'd been through a lot of small scrapes before.

On my portage past the most dangerous section of Crooked Chute, it became obvious that I had brought far too much unnecessary stuff, such as lots of extra clothes, food and equipment. Instead of my usual two trips down the half-kilometre last section of the portage trail, it took three to carry everything: one for the canoe, and two for the heavy gear. Also, I didn't follow my usual custom of stopping to sit beside the big chute itself after walking back up the trail once my first load was down, to rest, eat, and relax for an hour or so, while watching the spectacle of the roaring water. Instead, I had felt the need to press on, and ate only a couple of bites between carries. By the time I arrived at Rollway, I was tired and hungry. It was supper time, usually a better time to make camp than to start running a long rapid. But these are paltry justifications for bad judgement.

Looking down at the Rollway ledge while I stood scouting near the little cross, I could see that on that day, nearly all the water from the entire width of the river was being funnelled into a single powerful V, which poured over a small opening in the ledge slightly left of centre. I also made note of a large rock that I would need to especially watch out for and avoid. It was clearly exposed to the air immediately below the drop. In higher water this boulder would be buried under waves. It looked as if it might pose a slight challenge this time, but I would be able to easily see it coming from my boat. I planned a quick sharp manoeuvre to the right, immediately after dropping over the V. That would get me past, no problem.

My biggest error was that I was lazy. After scouting, I decided I wouldn't bother taking the time and trouble to carry my two loads of heavy gear down the portage, and leave it waiting at the end. Portaging all that would have allowed me to run the rapids with my boat almost empty, and therefore quite a bit lighter and more maneuverable. But the trail was almost a kilometre long. I was tired, and confident that I could navigate the run just fine, the way I had on previous trips. It seemed the easy way to save a lot of time and energy. I would just paddle my fully loaded canoe all the way down.

Other errors included not paying proper respect to the inherent risks that are always present whenever travelling solo, especially in a remote area. Also, although it was still full summer and would be light for a few hours, it was late in the day for me. But a particular destination had been pulling hard on my heart. I wanted to make it to my favourite campsite on the river: the big one by the high Natch Cliffs. I knew if I just kept going, I would get there in another hour or so. That specific site, and the whole gorgeous area surrounding it, is such a special place, almost a sanctuary. Whenever I had been blessed to camp there before, it had been a very memorable time, an extremely positive experience.

I decided supper, setting up camp, and resting could all wait, just a little. Then I would be able to enjoy the remainder of the evening at that five-star campsite, and sleep once again near the base of those stunning, 100-metre-high, grey and orange cliffs. I imagined that when I arrived, I might hear ravens croaking softly to each other high on the rock faces. As I fell asleep, there would perhaps be a light wind whispering in the giant pines. I would wake up the next morning, crawl out of my tent, and take in the splendid view. After a slow breakfast and maybe a swim, I would probably hike up the obscure steep trail to the very top of those cliffs, and the wonderful place I call Lookout Rock. There, I would be able to stand, feeling awed, fortunate and privileged, like a king or chief, soaking in the stunning panoramas up and down the river, gazing far down to the water, the campsite, and across the canyon to the cliffs on the far side.

It seems as if that whole area is rich with some sort of mystical power. In my mind, the big Natch Cliffs campsite is no ordinary place: it's a touchstone. As campsites go, it's as good as they get. I thought I might even spend two nights! So what if I was rushing a little, pushing a bit after a long day, in very low water conditions, alone? Also, it was raining a little. Still, all these factors combined are insufficient excuses.

As I've often told students on my Outdoor Ed trips, "When there are too many lemons, we walk." In other words, when the number of risk factors adds up to a large number, we portage! I learned this maxim about risk management early in my whitewater paddling days from experienced trippers. But, with no-one there to look after except myself, I didn't follow the rule. Lemons and all, I kept my gear with me in the canoe, and started down the rapids.

3

Steering through the first 400-metre section of complex whitewater, upriver from the river-crossing ledge, I was pleased. It was fun to zigzag around the boulders and find clear narrow channels. Right at the start, I even held up one hand on the fly and took a photograph with my digital camera. Now, I wince at the memory.

After steering the canoe so that it lined up in the exact right place, on mid river-left, I dropped her perfectly over that V in the wide ledge, then made my immediate 90° tight right turn. This went exactly the way I had planned, so that I avoided the large exposed boulder I had seen while scouting. However, with my boat momentarily perpendicular to the funnelled, concentrated current, I suddenly realized, with immediate urgent concern, that there was another, unexpected large boulder coming up fast!

I hadn't seen this second one during my scouting. Maybe it wasn't even visible from shore, I don't know. Perhaps I hadn't looked carefully enough, and didn't recognize its telltail splashes or the wave pattern. But from the angle at which I was presently flying across, the top of this second obstacle could definitely be seen. It was popping in and out of the surging water, just to the right of the first rock, and directly in my path. There was less than a boat-width between the two boulders, which meant there was no opening my canoe could squeeze through.

With a split-second to manoeuvre, my only option was to paddle hard and fast, power the boat further to the right, and get beyond the second rock before I hit it. But trying to do this meant keeping the canoe dangerously perpendicular to the mini-waterfall, the edge of the V. That water pushed hard from my immediate right, and also from behind. Because of the funnelling effect of the low water, the V contained most of the water coming down the river. And since it had just spilled over the ledge, much of it was surging and churning, full of air.

Paddling an open canoe perpendicular to a strong current of aerated water, is no place to linger. I pulled hard and fast on the paddle while trying to tilt the canoe downriver, to the left, away from the push. Tilting away from the direction of the oncoming current is the required manoeuvre in this kind of situation, in order to prevent the bucket-filling phenomenon. But this time, I wasn't able to do it for long, because in a couple of heartbeats the bottom of my canoe made solid contact with that second rock.

The left side rode up onto it, and stuck hard. In a boat without heavy gear, I'm sure I could have just shifted my weight and been able to shunt it immediately off the rock. Failing that, by lifting with my right knee I would have been able to tilt a lighter boat further to the left, in the safe downstream direction. Then I could have shoved my weight forward quickly a few times, and probably successfully humped the boat off the rock to freedom. Perhaps a more expert paddler might have had other solutions. I desperately did my best.

Though I had performed this kind of self-rescue move successfully many times, this time, it wasn't going to happen. I should have portaged the gear! The canoe stuck, and despite my strongest efforts, wouldn't slide off. Instead, surges of the current pushed the left side of the hull up even higher onto the boulder. I knew what this would mean. Having the left side pushed high on the rock, meant that the other side was being forced down. Down into the incoming rushing water. I couldn't stop it.

Water poured over the lower gunwale, flooding the boat and pushing the low side even further into the river. The boat filled immediately. The power of the river kept pushing, and in moments, huge spouts gushed from the upward mid-side and bow. The canoe was forced completely sideways, her top facing the current like a wide-open mouth, with the power of several fire hoses blasting in.

Crystal clear memories flashed of my Mountain River ordeal. The river would take her. I knew it would. I remembered the cross. Frantically shifting my weight repeatedly in the few seconds before it would be too late, I again tried desperately to hump the boat off the rock. But I already knew, right to my core. My boat was lost. Just like that.

There are laws of hydraulics that can't be denied or willed away. And there are limits to the physical strength of even a tough ABS plastic canoe. The steadily increasing weight and force of the incoming water relentlessly bent her hull backwards, breaching it, starting to turn it inside out. Above the roar of water surrounding me, I listened and stared as my prized wood gunwales splintered into pieces.

The two bolts on the lower side of the wooden deep-dish centre yoke suddenly popped loose from the broken gunwales, leaving it to wave around in the spray right in front of me like a crazy wooden arm. Kneeling in the flooded stern, with my hands glued to my paddle, the water had risen almost to my waist and wasn't going to stop there. She was definitely pinned. I had to go, and go fast.

Keeping hold of my paddle, I clutched the side of the canoe and spilled out into the river. At first the powerful current took my body and waved everything except my hands and arms as if I was a floppy rag doll. My legs were forced horizontal, and flapped in the downriver direction like a flag in a stiff wind. After a few seconds, I managed to pull my feet down, and achieve a tentative careful foothold on the river-bottom rocks. By some grace, the depth of the pulsing river that day was tailor-made for my height. I was able to stand with my head and neck just above the surface. This is a notoriously dangerous thing to do in fast water. Among other things it risks deadly foot entrapment, followed by drowning. I didn't have a choice.

Once standing, in a wobbly sort of way, I kept a strong hold on the side of the breached boat with one hand, while I unclipped a few carabineers. Using my PFD knife, I cut the tether line. This freed the gear. I grabbed a few items before everything washed out, then, with my back being pummelled, watched as the rest floated off down the river and around the next corner like a little parade. But this lessening of my boat's load had come too late. My canoe was bent completely backwards, solidly wrapped around the boulder like a red and grey banana peel.

Turning to lean forward into the torrent, I struggled to keep standing, and briefly imagined losing my balance and being swept away, bouncing through the remaining long string of boulders like my gear. Except I wouldn't float as high, and perhaps not at all. My trusty wooden guide's paddle, with its strong Kevlar-tipped blade and reinforced shaft, served me well as a staff. Feathering its blade to the current, I was able to wedge it between slippery unseen rocks on the bottom, giving me something to hold onto. With one hand clutching my salvage and the curved T-grip handle of the paddle, and the other gripping the canoe, my mind raced.

Glancing upward to the high river-right shore, I realized I was looking at the place where the small cross was located. This was perhaps the spot in the river, the exact spot, where a man had died. A sobering thought indeed.

It's a wonder to me how, in times of crisis, our bodies, brains and spirits can often rally. We yank priorities around, use a positive, determined mind set and increased effort, and suddenly feel a jolt of hope and strength. Looking up from my spread-eagled scarecrow stance in the river I felt that positive burst and told myself firmly, "I'm not going to die here! I'm going to make it home to my family." Splashes of water doused my face.

All my experience and knowledge funnelled into a few seconds of planning. With heaving water pushing repeatedly on my chest and neck, I remembered the obvious-sounding instruction, often forgotten in such circumstances, and kept my mouth closed. For only a couple of seconds did I consider intentionally letting go, and just allowing my body to float through, in the so-called "go-cart position," with my feet held high in front and my bum up, to reduce the risk of impact on rocks. But in the present situation, it would be quite a dangerous float, because of the long series of big boulders still left. Unlike my buoyant bobbing gear, I would probably be smashed around repeatedly, and possibly knocked unconscious. My drowning body might easily become trapped somewhere down deep. Again, I thought of the cross and a fellow paddler who just didn't make it. No, floating through would be my last resort, to be done only if unavoidable or accidental.

I committed to bracing on the bottom with my paddle and slowly, carefully, walking through the neck deep rushing water to the closest land. This meant traversing roughly three or four metres (12 feet) through the river, to reach the river-right side of the ledge. Once there, I would pull myself out and be safe.

But first I had to think. What needed to be done before I let go of the canoe? Thankfully the summer water was warm, and the day mild. Still, I knew hypothermia and exhaustion would quickly overtake me if I stayed immersed much longer. I was also at high risk of breaking an ankle, getting a foot caught, and other nightmare scenarios. Dark thoughts and fears washed over me again.

When I first stepped into the river and untethered the gear, I had pulled out, to keep with me, the big blue plastic food barrel, my spare paddle, and my red teardrop day-pack. Inside the day-pack were a few special items, some of which I had waterproofed in zip-lock plastic bags. These were things I wanted to have close at hand on the trip, and a few valuables. Just after pulling that red bag out, with my water bottle clipped to it, I was standing facing upriver, clinging to the canoe and spare paddle with one hand, and the bobbing barrel, my guide's paddle, and the handle strap of the day-pack in the other. Almost immediately the force of the current, as if alive, tore open the main top zipper of my pack, and dumped most of its contents into the moving water. With no free hand to stop them, I watched with dismay as those zip-lock bags floated away down the froth line, another little parade. They too disappeared around the next corner. Zip-locks are famous for popping open and leaking in such situations. Then, of course, weighed down by their contents, they sink. But there was no point in self-admonishments while standing in the middle of the river. I knew my survival depended on focussing on the positive, the now, and on getting out of the river quickly.

I consolidated my grip on everything. But before leaving, I needed to somehow get hold of the loose ends of the two five-metre long (16.5 feet) floating painter ropes that were tied to the bow and stern of the canoe. Using the handle and shaft of my spare aluminum paddle I was able to fish them both in. Then, holding their ends, the handle of the heavy floating food barrel, what was left of my burst day-pack, and the spare paddle in one hand, I started to walk. My right hand, holding the salvage, was being yanked and tugged furiously behind me, as I led with the guide's paddle in my left. Slowly and carefully, I stepped away, and left my canoe.

Shaking off fear and nostalgic sentiment, I glanced up at the sky. At that precise moment, for a few precious seconds, a flock of little birds flew in a lilting way across the river, right over my head. I surprised myself by smiling. Life goes on! There's always beauty somewhere close by, even in times of great difficulty. For a few moments, I stopped and let this vision lift my spirit and inspire me. Somehow it gave me hope. Then pulling my eyes back to the surface of the water, I returned to the task. But those little birds would not be forgotten.

In ultra-slow motion, I took tiny heal-to-toe steps through the torrent. Everything on my trailing arm bounced around and pulled hard. I was ready to let it all go in an instant if my feet started to slip. Keeping the blade of my guide's paddle knife-edged to the flow, I used it to brace on the bottom, as I tentatively, blindly pushed on each riverbed rock with my foot, before transferring my weight. Continuously buffeted and blasted by the current, I felt like a sky-diver, with my clothes flapping in the wind. Except this was a horizontal gale of water.

It seems odd, but in the midst of crossing, I couldn't help thinking of how incredibly blessed my life was. I also knew that somehow, I would make it home to my loved ones. At this moment, it was all I wanted to do. There was turmoil surrounding me, yet a feeling of grace inside. I was lucky to have a home, and loved ones to return to. Very few other things really matter. As I kept up my bizarre form of water-walking, the river continued pumping high-speed, yet everything began to seem slowed down, intense, and sharply focussed. One step at a time.

At last, my fingers reached out and grabbed hold of the warm, black, smooth lip of the ledge. Relief and gratitude flooded through me. It was the edge of the river-right shore. Hauling my body and gear out, I must have looked like some primeval creature, emerging from the deep.

Still holding the ends of the two lines, I crawled a step, then immediately turned around and lay flat on my back, knees up and arms straight out to the sides, exhausted. That rock bed felt so perfect. It had been sculpted smooth by the river over the ages. Plus, on that day, the earlier afternoon sun had made it deliciously warm! My back, arms and palms soaked in the sensation of contact, and I rested quietly for several minutes. I said my inner thanks. In higher water, this section of the riverbed would have been under fast flowing water, perched at the brink of a wide mini-waterfall caused by the river-crossing ledge. But on this memorable day, I was on safe, dry land, with that big rushing V pouring over the opening in the ledge just to my left. I lay as if in a trance, while the chute sang its white noise song.

A quick self-assessment told me I was unhurt. Though extremely tired, I still had some strength. Nothing was broken. The two painter ropes were still tied to the boat, and the other ends were in my hand. It had even stopped raining for the time being. There would be a couple of hours of daylight left before pitch dark. In that time, I would be able to hike down-river and try to recover my gear. I was sound and whole. Life cannot be replaced. I would be a lucky one.

After reviving a bit, I stood up on the dry, flat riverbed rock and gave a couple of hard, but predictably useless, tugs on the ropes. This confirmed what I already knew. Ropes weren't going to budge any part of this boat, against the constant over-whelming power of the river. She wasn't going to come off that rock by any human power, even with Z-drag lines, pulleys and ten strong paddlers.

As this sank in, I closed my eyes and lowered my head. That boat and I had been together a long time: fourteen years since I bought her new in June of 1991, shortly before leav-ing Ottawa and flying north to do our Mountain River trip in rental boats. I knew how she had received almost every major scratch on her hull and dent on her gunwales. She had taken me to countless places. We had many, many good times together. If it is possible for a boat to be a friend, that canoe was my friend. Now it hurt to look at her.

I rallied, and tied the ends of the lines to the bedrock, then moved all the salvaged gear to a secure place beside the bottom of the high bank for later pick up. After a last look, I picked up my guide's paddle, my trusty staff. There was noth-ing more to do. Maybe later. I scrambled up the riverbank to the portage trail and started walking downriver.

End of the Portage

4

Hiking any distance in thin soggy paddling shoes is not recommended. They're designed for stepping in or out of a boat in the shallows, finding footholds while in the water, and only small amounts of shore walking. Some have good tread, thickness, and ankle support. Mine had almost none. Ballet slippers would probably have given the same protection. At least both of them were still on my feet as I hurried along the trail, repeatedly climbing down and back up the bank, searching for gear.

The big barrel had come with me from the boat, so I knew I would at least be able to eat. But I needed to find my tent and large waterproof canoe pack. The big bag had been floating high when it bobbed off down the river, but I was very worried that my little tent, not strapped to anything, might have sunk, and be lost.

There were, of course, still lots of lemons. My troubles would get much worse if I injured myself. Although still pumped with adrenalin, my fatigue was growing, and with it, the beginnings of desperation. Time and again, I would look for salvage in places that looked like good prospects, only to find nothing. Discouraged, even fatalistic thoughts, began crossing my mind as the reality of my isolation sank in. But there was no time for that! I knew my search had to be completed quickly, before everything floated further away, beyond my limited hiking range, or sank. Full darkness would soon make finding anything impossible.

Finally, when I got to the very bottom of the portage trail, I looked across the river to the far side and shouted with delight. Just past the end of the rapids, where the water becomes much deeper and calmer, I saw my turquoise canoe pack floating in a large, slow-swirling shore eddy. Although I would have to swim about seven metres (23 feet) across to river-left to retrieve it, I knew this would gain me dry clothes, my dry sleeping bag, my Therm-a-Rest inflatable mattress, and many other wonderful supplies. Still wearing my PFD, as I had throughout my search for both safety and warmth, I stopped and double-checked its zipper, straps, carabiner clips, knife and waist tie-string. Leaving my paddle leaning against a large boulder by the shore, I swallowed my discomfort, closed my mouth, and waded back in.

Though still flowing fairly quickly, the river is safer there because it is so much deeper, as it flows into a long section of quieter water. This time my feet were thankfully nowhere near the bottom, and I enjoyed the feeling of buoyancy as I swam easily across to the big friendly eddy.

Grabbing a strap, I pulled the pack toward me and was thrilled to see it was undamaged. After towing the bag to the shallows at the edge of the eddy, I climbed out and hauled it onto dry land, making doubly sure it wouldn't roll back in and float away. I then stood and carefully scanned the full length and width of the eddy, looking on the surface and also deep into the dark green, almost black water. Was there anything else?

Another bolt of excitement exploded as I spotted my tent! It was at the far end of the eddy, only a couple of metres off-shore, in deep water, and practically invisible, due to being almost fully submerged and its dark beige colour. Everything except a corner of one end of the bag was hanging straight down. Thankfully a little air remained trapped in the nylon sack, and was keeping it afloat, but just barely. It looked as if it might sink any second. Grabbing a long branch from shore, I reached out and fished in the prize. It too was undamaged! I was flooded with relief and gratitude, knowing I would be able to not only eat, but also have both my sleeping bag and my tent to sleep in that night!

After a final scan, I clipped my treasures together using a carabiner from my PFD, waded into the river again and, towing them, swam back across to river-right. Once ashore at the end of the portage trail, I smiled across at that wonderful eddy, and said my inner thanks again. As I did so, my joy was somewhat dampened when I realized that eddy might perhaps have been where Blair Fraser's body had washed out.

Conscious of having limited daylight and energy left, I loaded myself up, grabbed my paddle, and went to work carrying my pack and tent up the trail to the small campsite that is located near the top of the rapids. It would be my base. A misty rain started again, but it didn't matter. I was drenched anyway.

Turning around and walking back down to the shore near the wreck for my second load, I retrieved the food barrel, day-pack, water bottle and spare paddle. The situation in the river hadn't changed at all. No surprise. But I was thankful to have recovered so much gear.

When I had finished hauling the last load to the trailhead campsite, and just before setting up the tent, I hiked all the way back down to the end of the portage one more time. From there, in the rapidly fading light, I carefully bushwhacked a little further down along the river-right shore, searching for the last few missing pieces of gear: those zip-lock bags with so-called valuables that had poured out of my daypack.

But they were gone, without a trace. No camera, no maps, no wallet. My little pocket calendar booklet was gone too. That day-planner was my portable memory bank. I have a complete set of these calendars, one for each of my 29 years of teaching, full of scribbled notes. Now, the one for 2004-2005 was gone forever. Lost were phone numbers, dates, reminders, birthdays, doctor's and dentist appointments – a year of supposedly important information.

Pushing myself to hike quickly back up to my refuge campsite before total darkness closed in, I kept telling myself this was all just stuff. Things that could be replaced. Any truly important information could be found again. And the rest? I would just have to let it go.

Self recriminations raged as I gathered together the driest twigs I could find, so that I would be able to get a little fire going. There would be no camping at the big Natch Cliffs campsite for me that night. I had seriously messed up on my scouting and judgement, was lucky just to be alive, and my prized canoe was wrecked.

Forcing myself to think more positively, I found comfort in the fact that I was quite a bit safer than I had been a few hours earlier. With the immediate urgency of the crisis subsiding, and feelings of personal safety growing, I was able to emotionally let go a bit, and allow anger and fear turn to sadness.

Complete cloudy darkness fell, and I dug out my candle lantern and small flashlight from the canoe pack. Thank goodness everything inside it was still bone dry, due to its giant drybag liner. I lit the little candle lantern, hooked it on a branch, then grabbed a few things from the food barrel. A reluctant smoky campfire was eventually persuaded to burn. Sitting beside it, I cooked a quick supper, ate, and felt better.

Roughly three hours after hitting the rock, I had my tent set up, and a dry bed waiting. Out of the river for the day, and with warm food inside, I again began appreciating my blessings. Just after 9:00, the light rain stopped so I changed into a complete set of clean dry clothes, including socks and hiking shoes. I also made a clothesline out of my throw-bag rope, and hung up my wet clothes. This included my white "Canada Rocks" T-shirt, with five Inuksuk on it, that I was wearing when I hit the rock. I smiled. 'Canada Rocks' indeed. Those five red Inuksuk in a vertical yellow column had always reminded me of my wonderful family of five. They did so again that night.

Once this was done, I had no choice but to immediately go and lie down. It was heaven to have a dry bed! Thank goodness for tents, canoe-packs lined with waterproof dry bags, Therm-a-rests, and quality sleeping bags. Especially, thank goodness that I was safe. Although the rain had stopped, my tent was still drenched all around me from its swim in the river. But I lay on a lovely dry island, created by the thin inflated mattress under my dry sleeping bag. I closed my eyes.

The waters of Rollway rumbled on loudly beside my tent. In some ways, I felt I was still in the river. My mind hadn't stopped flying around, continuously reassessing the situation, weighing options. Still, the singing of a few evening birds after the rain gave me great comfort.

Although exhausted, I didn't sleep well. Usually the night sounds of rapids near my tent are a soothing lullaby. But that night, their white noise sounds triggered repeated sensory flashes of being up to my neck and beyond, in pounding water.

Sensations surged though me of the many worse catastrophes that could have happened.

During the most difficult hours, I repeatedly lurched awake from terrifying dreams in a panic. Not aware I had even fallen asleep, I would yank myself away from vivid mental scenes where I was caught beneath the surface of rushing, foaming water, terrified, thrashing, frantically flailing about, out of control, trapped. Sometimes my body was pinned against a rock, broken like my boat. Sometimes I was desperately trying to swim upward, to get away from some deep deadly darkness. But I couldn't escape. There was no escape. I was drowning. Fighting to get to the surface, to breath. I couldn't make it. I was going to die, and saw bubbles rising from my mouth and nostrils, up into the froth as blackness descended and my brain lost consciousness. Then I would lurch awake. Several times I switched on my little flashlight and looked around the tent to remind myself that I really was okay. Eventually I would shake off the fright and fall back asleep, only to have the same nightmare again.

It seems like it's only when the most frightening pivotal point in a crisis has passed that we allow ourselves to imagine the worst that could have happened. That night I was so very thankful to be alive and physically sound. Safe in my bed, I again thanked the river, the Great Spirit, the Lord, my blind luck, everything.

5

Morning is my favourite time of day, especially when I'm outside in wild places. The light returns. There's a feeling of a fresh start. I usually have renewed energy and a clearer head. It's a time when I often do a lot of productive thinking. That Rollway new morning was quite a bit better than usual. Despite the rough night, the errors of the previous day, their serious consequences, and complaints from my aching body, I woke up feeling revitalized and inspired in a way I had only ever experienced once before. That had been on my Mountain River trip, just after I leapt to shore and safety from the rock where our wrapped canoe was pinned. Probably it was connected to coming close to dying.

As I crawled out of my little tent by the Petawawa, the sun was shining and a beautiful day greeted me. The rushing river, brilliant sky, jewel drops of morning dew, twittering birds, glistening spider webs, and the soft, gently swaying arms of the evergreens, indeed all of nature seemed perfect on that morning after. Even the very air and ground beneath my feet seemed precious. My thoughts waxed philosophical again as I ate a big breakfast. Each new day *is* magic. Everything gets a chance to somehow start again. It was surely going to be a difficult day, but I was feeling positive.

I hung a few more things on the line to air and dry, while mentally going over my resources and options. My most significant loss wasn't my wallet. Credit cards and cash are a bother to replace, but would all get done in time. Copies of most of my lost family photos and phone numbers could probably be found and reprinted or updated. In a month, all of those sorts of things would be back to normal.

My digital camera was also gone, but so what? It was a cheap early model, considered old tech. It would be good to buy a new one. The downside was, I would never get to see that cock-sure last picture I had snapped on the fly at the start of what I thought was a safe run. That lost little pocket calendar book was full of old information I didn't really need any more.

No, the most significant loss was my collection of maps.[2] They had been stored in one of those handy zip-lock bags that spewed out of my burst day-pack. I made a mental note: always bring back-up copies of maps, packed in either the waterproof canoe-pack or in the barrel, just in case.

Because I had paddled this river a few times before, I knew this section of the canoe route pretty well. But that didn't mean I would be able to find my way if I left the river and tried to hike out ten, or who knows, maybe twenty kilometres through the bush. If I couldn't get my boat off the rock today, and that seemed probable, I would have to find some other way to reach the main park road on foot. Once there, I could hitch-hike back to my car at the Lake Travers parking

2 This included copies of both the PETAWAWA RIVER Whitewater Guide, Algonquin Provincial Park, by George Drought, and the Algonquin Park CANOE ROUTES map.

lot. First, retrieving the canoe would be given my very best try, but my heart already knew it was a lost cause. Maps would have helped with planning, but I had none.

My options narrowed to four:

1. Somehow get the boat off, repair it, and paddle out by myself as originally planned, to the end of the trip at McManus Lake, roughly 27 kilometres away. This was extremely unlikely.

2. Hitch a ride down the river with others who might come along. This was not a great option, and probably unsafe. My extra bulk and weight would be a huge imposition on them, and dramatically increase their workload and personal risk. There were still several more rapids to ride through, in what would be a very overloaded boat.

3. Walk out cross-country through the forest to the main park road, then hitch-hike to my car. Thank goodness I still had the keys, securely clipped inside my PFD pocket as always. It would probably be a very difficult and danger-ous hike, bush-whacking, especially without a map. There would be a high risk of getting lost or injured. It would be arduous, with an uncertain outcome. Lots of lemons.

4. Or, I could somehow hitch a ride in a passing canoe back up the river a short way, to the little refurbished historic log ranger cabin located by the water, just below the outwash of Crooked Chute, the last big rapids. As I had passed the cabin, I noticed that a small bush road ends there, right beside the cabin. It would surely lead out to the main park road. If I could just get back to that cabin, and walk along the bush road to the main park road, I could hitchhike to my car. Then I could drive it back down that old bush road to the cabin, and pick up my gear. Possibly this was my best option. But it depended on someone coming along

the portage trail. And they would need to have room in their boat, and be kind. It was midweek, and given the lateness in the season and the extreme low water, I had seen no-one.

After breakfast, I walked a hundred metres from my tent to the yellow Algonquin Park head-of-the-portage sign. Using duct tape, I attached to it the most visible warning sign I could make. In large letters on a sheet of paper ripped from my sketch book it said, "Danger! Don't run! Wrecked boat in river." I was afraid another paddler might come along, without knowing what lay ahead. If they didn't get out at that portage sign and scout the rapids, they would run smack into my ropes and canoe, almost certainly clothesline themselves, and dump.

Turning and going part way down the portage, I discovered a small rough bush track branching off to the right. From an exploratory 15-minute walk, I learned I could probably hike along there quite a long way. Maybe I might even be able to follow it and eventually get to the main park road. But realistically, I would not. Especially without maps, it would be unsafe. Fallen and leaning trees blocked the way in many places, and despite the summer dryness of the forest, shallow water flooded it in several sections. With time, effort and skill, a person on an ATV might have driven along there sometime in the past, but now they would need to be packing a chain saw. Trying to travel all that way alone, on foot, tired and slugging my heavy gear, I would likely get lost, hurt, or both. Being such a long way off the main canoe route, no help would come. "Don't make things worse!" and other cautions and safety procedures rang in my ears. I hiked back to the main trail, and turned right.

A little further down the portage I returned to the scene. In the bright morning sunshine, the view from the high riverbank looked much the same as the evening before. Although such a discouraging sight, it came as no surprise. My poor Mad River was still welded to the rock. No overnight magic had occurred. It hadn't shifted in the slightest, and wasn't going to.

Anyone who has ever loved a boat and lost it, knows how deeply the loss can be felt. Struggling with acceptance, I knew I had no realistic hope of freeing her. This time standing quietly, I didn't focus on my stupidity. I just allowed myself to feel sad.

After a few minutes, I continued to the bottom of the trail and looked one more time for missing gear. No surprises there either. After hiking back to the scene again, this time I climbed down the riverbank and walked across the smooth, black, dry river-bottom. The powerful V poured down to the left just as strongly, and the full weight of the river still kept the canoe's bow and stern lines taunt. I hauled on each rope, just in case, but knew before doing it nothing was going to budge. They were arrow-straight lines, yellow lasers shooting through the air, pointing to the two submerged open ends of the canoe and disappearing in fountains of spray. I had planted her right near the middle of the strongest, most concentrated current. And despite the dryness and low water level, the Petawawa is always a mighty river.

Feeling the tightness of those ropes, I knew for certain this boat was not going to rise again. She would not be coming off that rock by any human force. For even some large group of people to be able to pull or pry, then haul whatever was left out of the water, they would have to somehow cut it, twist it, and probably rip it apart. No, my old Mad River would only come off when the river itself rose higher and floated it off. Some future flood waters would have to lift and move it. She would still be a wreck then, flattened, torn, broken, but at least free. I knew I wouldn't be there to see it.

To my surprise, at this moment of giving up, my determination made a sudden quantum shift. I decided I would have to do it myself, metaphorically. I would personally rise again: get out of there safely, get another boat, come back someday, and finish the trip. I told myself, "There's more than one way to rise again!" I wouldn't allow this loss to defeat my spirit, or ruin my lifelong love of wild nature and canoeing.

As this surge of bravado rushed through me, I noticed that the sparkling rapids looked quite beautiful. The river wasn't to blame, I was. Lined with graceful trees, the water flowed on. Those white horses hopped and splashed. Yes, the river is always the same, yet always changing, a little bit different every day – sometimes a lot different. I counselled myself to appreciate at least part of each day more, even during times of adversity, sadness, and loss.

Letting go has never been a strong point for me. It's both a strength and a weakness. I seem to make strong emotional bonds with only a few people and things, even places, then tend to cling to them, even sometimes when reason calls me a fool. I decided to climb back up the bank and walk down the trail to the viewpoint by the cross once more, to make a final assessment. Predictably, from there the prognosis was no better. There was no way to rescue her. I, on the other hand, was able to move on. I needed to leave, and began emotionally preparing myself.

However, while wrestling with the reality of going, I couldn't help worrying about the serious danger to navigation my boat and those ropes would present to people who would eventually come down the river. My conscience and a strong sense of responsibility to others told me I couldn't just leave such a hazard out there, close to the heavily travelled V, waiting to injure people. I reasoned that, if pulling the boat off and repairing it, was indeed hopeless, and if it truly was irretrievable by anyone, then maybe, for the safety of future paddlers, I should at least try to prevent it from blocking the path below the V before I go. With another rush of bravado, which this time was more than a little crazy, I decided it was my duty to try and cut the canoe's hull in two, and clear it from the river.

My folding triangular camp saw from the barrel would do the job. This time the lines would be out there for me to hold on to. Strong with the faith and coffee of the new morning, I formed a quick plan. Carrying the saw, I would hold tight to one of the ropes, and walk very carefully back through the river, return to the boat, and cut it to pieces. Later this would seem incredibly foolish. It most certainly was. But at the time I believed it might save lives.

I hurried up from the cross to the campsite and gathered a few things. Then, wearing only my shorts, a T-shirt, water-shoes and my PFD, I went back along the trail and scampered down the high bank to the dry ledge, armed with my trusty paddle, the assembled saw, and a full set of dry clothes. After leaving the clothes at the bottom of the bank, I strode over to the exact spot where I had hauled myself out the day before.

Taking hold of one rope, I sat down on the lip of the ledge, with my feet in the water. Leading with the paddle blade, I poked it down into the moving water until it touched the bottom, ready to feel its way again. With my determination strong, I held the saw in my other hand and slipped into the river. The water again surged to my neck. But this time I had the tight line to hold. After a furtive glance up to the location of the cross, I carefully retraced my steps, and slowly made my way back to the very middle of it all, back to my boat.

Things were still grim. Bracing on the handle of the paddle, with its blade and my feet planted as firmly as possible on the river-bottom rocks, I stood touching the side of the canoe and turned my body slightly, trying to use it to deflect some of the pressure from the current. With the flow pounding hard on my back, I grabbed the stern end of the hull and hauled on it with all my might. Twice. This had absolutely no effect. I just needed to try.

Then I began my grisly task. Holding the boat and paddle with one hand, I angled the saw with the other so it bit into the high side, near the place mid-ship where the ABS plastic had already started to rip from grinding on the rock. It takes a lot to rip that stuff. In the middle of the red outside of the boat, just below the wood gunwale, in white decal letters, are printed the manufacturer's logo words "Mad River Canoe." I had often used that middle letter V as a guide to line up the balance, or pivot point, the exact centre of the boat where the carrying yoke is fastened. Although I couldn't see the words as I stood in the river looking at the grey insides of the boat, I knew where they were. My saw started cutting down into the side of the hull, roughly a hand span before the word Mad.

My intent was to enable the boat to wash away in pieces down the river, but this was not to be. While struggling in the fray I became increasingly aware of the huge risk I was taking. After fifteen frightening minutes, I had only achieved a 25 centimetre (10 inch) saw-cut down into the plastic, and my saw hand was now fully submerged, trying unsuccessfully to work in the strong turbulence under the surface. As the blade began to round the corner from the side of the canoe into the bottom, it kept bouncing, wildly twisting and turning, getting nowhere. It was impossible. Too dangerous!

I surrendered to the truth. I wasn't going to be able to lift my canoe off, pull it off, or even cut it off. She would have to stay in the river. Defeated, but resolute, I knew what had to be done. Abandon the boat!

Just before carefully stepping away, I made a last decision, and grabbed hold of my beautiful deep-dish centre yoke. That well-used piece of finely sculpted wood had rested on my neck countless times as I portaged. Now attached to only one side of the boat by the two remaining bolts, it was still waving around erratically in the spray like a demented wooden arm, as it had since immediately after the wreck. If I couldn't take my boat with me, I could at least take this! I leaned against the canoe, and holding the butt of the paddle under my armpit, used both hands to grip the yoke. After twisting it back and forth several times, the wood of the remaining gunwale it was fastened to finally gave way. The yoke came off in my hands. I would bring it home.

Cautiously retracing my water-walk, I came back to the dry lip of shore, and climbed out. For another few moments, I stood there dripping, looking, thinking. Holding my saw, paddle, and yoke, I was remembering. Saying goodbye. I looked around in the sky for any flock of those little birds, but there were none.

Drenched, but quickly warmed by the mid-morning sun, I folded up the saw, no-traced-the-place the best I could, and walked back across the smooth black rock to my little pile of dry clothes. There was nothing more I could do. I would leave the boat and the ropes, walk back up the portage trail, pack up camp, and try to figure out what to do next.

End of the Portage

6

I stripped and started to change.

Sometimes life can give you such a good laugh! There I was, completely naked, wobbling on one foot, struggling to pull on my first sock, when I looked up and saw, only a few metres away on the portage trail, two men walking down. They had, of course, already seen me.

Overjoyed to see someone, I shouted a welcoming "Hello!" One of them called back, probably with his tongue in his cheek, "Having a bit of trouble?" No answer was needed. Standing there dressed in only a sock, I realized I must look pretty funny. Neither of them cracked a visible smile, though they must have been stifling themselves. I laughed out loud. I had been humbled, could have been severely injured or killed, my boat was a wreck, and now had to be abandoned. But there I stood, literally "em-bare-assed." I dressed in a flash, grabbed everything, and scuttled up the bank to meet them.

You have to wonder what people might think in a situation like this. However, these paddlers were polite and kind. They were travelling in one canoe, and had done so on similar trips in other years. Their boat was pulled up on the riverside at the head of the trail, and they were presently in the process of wisely portaging all their gear to the end of Rollway. They were then going to return and carry their canoe down as well. They had seen my warning at the trailhead sign, but had already planned to portage. They had also seen my little tent site. After hearing a quick summary of my story as we stood looking out at the pinned boat, they asked what I planned to do.

I find it hard to ask strangers for help. But sometimes there's just no other way, and people are basically good. Winter drivers who see another car stuck in the snow will nearly always stop and give a push. They become unsung highway heroes. In the same way, paddlers almost universally help each other. These two kind men did this for me, and I remain forever grateful.

Meekly, I told them my tentative plan, that it looked like my only safe option was to hitch a ride with all my gear in "someone's" boat, and go back up the river to the old ranger cabin at the bottom of Crooked Chute. Although this meant traveling up-current a couple of kilometres, the flow would be gentle, mainly flatwater with only one short swift. I said I would be happy to carry the boat up that portage. Once back at the cabin, I could be left alone, and whoever gave me a lift could then continue on back downriver with their trip. I would camp the night there, and hike out to the main park road in the morning. When I got to the road, I would hitch-hike to my car at the Lake Travers parking area, then drive back down the bush road, and pick up my gear.

They had a map! This confirmed that the paddle upriver would be only two kilometres, and the bush road hike about nine. Though I hated to interrupt their trip, I humbly asked if they could help me out. Without a moment's hesitation, they said they would do it!

They asked how long it would take me to pack up. Thrilled with my good luck, I said, "Only twenty minutes." After saying

I should take my time, and not rush on their account, they continued off down the portage to leave their gear at the end. Feeling guilty, but tremendously relieved and full of hope, I dashed up the trail and packed.

Just before going to bed the night before, over my little supper fire I had dried a piece of sweetgrass braid. I almost always carry some in a plastic bag in my PFD pocket. It means quite a lot to me. Respectfully I had burned a little and let the smoke wash over me. When I was set to carry my last load to my new friends' canoe, I stopped for a moment. Ready to paddle, and wearing my still-wet PFD, I took the braid from the plastic bag in the pocket again and unclipped my PFD knife from its holder. I cut a short piece from the remaining braid, and left it on one of the fire circle rocks. For the next person.

Once all my stuff had been loaded into their waiting boat, I asked the two men one more favour. There was something I had to do. Would they please wait for me fifteen more minutes? Leaving them puzzled beside their boat, I rushed down the portage trail a final time to the riverside bank closest to the canoe. Scurrying down, I hurried across the dry black ledge. Rallying my resolve, I pulled out my PFD knife. Reaching out as far as I dared over the rushing water toward the ruined canoe, I did my final act of separation, and cut the lines. Contact was broken.

There would be no retrieving the canoe, but at least there would be no future clothes-lining. Although it was still quite a dangerous situation out there, hopefully a boat could now get safely past without hitting the wreck. From my vantage point, a very narrow line of travel looked open. As a canoe or kayak dropped through the V, it would have to go slightly left of that first big exposed rock instead of right, and skim past its far side. They would also have to do several quick manoeuvres through the remaining big rocks of the run. I tried to convince myself that a skilled paddler, in an unloaded boat, would probably be able to make it. It was the best I could do. I scrambled up the bank, and ran up to the trailhead. My ride was waiting. I was on my way home.

Just before the three of us got into their canoe, which was empty except for my gear, these two river heroes smiled and handed me forty dollars! They said that since I had lost my wallet, I would need the money to buy gas and food on my way home. How incredibly thoughtful and decent of them. I hadn't even thought of this part of my troubles. I gratefully accepted, and got the phone number and address of one of them so I could repay them once I got home. We all got in and pushed off.

Paddling upriver isn't something done very often these days. Most people don't even think about it. Yet in the days when First Nations paddlers were the only canoe travellers, they created and used portage trails as ways to go both up and down difficult sections of a river. We would only need to go up one, at the swift, on our way back to the bottom of Crooked Chute.

At the 200-metre portage, I got out and carried my gear in two loads while the two men lined their empty canoe along the river's edge, past the swift. In total, it took us only an hour to get back to the old cabin. I quickly unloaded my gear and thanked them again profusely for helping me out, and for delaying their trip. I pored over the map one last time, then smiled and waved goodbye as they paddled away downriver, to finish their trip. So far so good.

The ranger cabin wasn't rented, but it was, of course, padlocked. So were the two upside-down Grumman canoes chained beside it. I made a small fire in the circle of stones near the river's edge, and started boiling water while I set up my little tent beside the end of the bush road. Though it was only mid-afternoon, I was quite ready for supper and bed, and was hoping for a much better sleep.

As I built the fire, I noticed a person moving about, over on the far side of the wide section of river in front of me that formed a kind of outwash lake after the long Crooked Chute rapid. They were only about 200 metres directly across the water. But surprisingly, I could see no boat sitting on that shore. How had they gotten there? A couple of bright glints near the person soon answered my question. The flashes must have been reflections from metal or glass, maybe from some kind of four-wheeled ATV parked in the trees over there. So, they had actually driven to that point. Hmmm...

The north boundary of Algonquin Park comes very close to Crooked Chute. This visitor, perhaps bending park rules a little, had apparently driven down a few kilometres, maybe from Mackey's Station or some other nearby community. My usual disrespect for people who break park rules was temporarily suspended due to the circumstances.

I thought, "This could be my ticket home!" I considered doing a long swim across, and asking for their help, but quickly decided against it. The swim could probably be done without much risk, since the water was calm, and of course I would wear my PFD. But I was quite tired. Also, I wouldn't be able to bring my gear. I sternly told myself to be more cautious. Enough of being in the river! Too many lemons! No, I would take the safer, self-rescue way, and hike out, as planned.

Less than an hour later, with my little camp in order, I had just started eating when suddenly a man walked up to me from the bottom of the Crooked Chute portage trail, the one I had hiked down with my three loads the day before. I thought he must be a river tripper with his canoe still up the trail. But once we had greeted and chatted, I learned he wasn't a portaging canoeist at all. He was the person I had seen moving around on the far side of the river, the driver of the ATV. He said he had come across to this side because he'd always wanted to get a good look at this old cabin.

With the river level so low, he said he had been able to actually walk across the whole river upstream of the main part of the Chute, rock-hopping all the way, and had only gotten wet to his thighs! I was stunned and puzzled to hear this, and thought it must surely have been dangerous. But there he stood. He said he'd driven into the park from the north as I thought, and would be returning home that evening.

I was happy to have his company and conversation, and told him a quick summary of my story. Then it was his turn to be surprised. He had brought a small bag with him and kindly offered me some food. I told him I had plenty, and could give him some of mine. We ate together around the fire, chatting, looking over his maps, and talking about my situation.

He asked if I there was any possible way my canoe might be rescued, maybe if a big enough group of people went down there with pulleys and lots of other equipment. I told him no, that even if an organized group did manage to peel the wreck off that rock and haul it onto shore, all they would get would be a flattened, inside-out, ripped, and saw-cut hull, with shattered gunwales and broken seats. It was irreparable. Someday the river would float or wash it off, perhaps after a big rain, or maybe in the spring. But I had detached myself, abandoned it, because in truth, no-one could save it.

I considered walking back across the top of the rapids with him and hitching a ride out on his ATV. He generously offered this, but I needed sleep. My little camp was all set up. I had a good plan to get myself safely home the next day. Most of all,

I didn't want to risk more water-walking. Best not to push my luck, or the river's good graces. Although it was heartwarming to again experience the generosity of strangers, I declined.

I did however take him up on his offer to phone someone for me when he got home. I asked him to call the Algonquin Portage store, located just outside the park on the Sand Lake-Achray-Lake Travers Road, to set up a shuttle pick-up with them. I would be hiking out along the bush road early in the morning, and so told him it would be great if he could arrange with them to pick me up at noon where it meets the main park road, near the big hydro tower corridor. Then I would at least have a guaranteed ride to get to my car at Lake Travers. By this time, I had also remembered that I had an additional twenty dollars, which I always keep in my Tilly hat. This would help with expenses. If needed, I was pretty sure the great people who own the store would accept credit from me under the circumstances. I wrote my message out for him, and he was happy to help.

Just before he left I requested one more favour. I added my home phone number to the piece of paper, and asked him to please wait until the night after next, then call it. If I was there at home, I would be happy to hear from him, and would tell him how my adventures had gone. But if I wasn't back, and this was something very hard for me to think about, I asked him to please tell my wife all the news that I had told him, and when and where he had last seen me. And that I loved her. I knew this was a morbid precaution, but I was still shaky. It had to be done, just in case.

He promised to make both calls, and stuffed the paper into his day-pack. We smiled, shook hands, and he walked away up the Crooked Chute portage, ready to rock-hop his way back to the far side, and drive home.

After eating two complete dehydrated meals, each supposedly good for two people, I felt comfortably full. But I wasn't able to crawl into my tent just yet, because twenty minutes later more surprise visitors showed up. First, I heard distant noises, then voices coming down the bush road. I was soon shocked to see three kids on mountain bikes emerge and pedal up right beside me. The oldest was a young teenager. None of them had much gear, only small backpacks. They were equally surprised to see me, camped beside the river with my little tent. The oldest explained that their fathers had rented the log cabin for a week, and their two dads were just a little way behind on the overgrown track. I asked if their fathers were driving a car in, while the three of them biked. They smiled and said, "Oh no, no-one could drive here on this old road. It's way too rough. And there's this big huge ditch thing right near the beginning. No car could drive past that." The news landed with a thud!

A few minutes later the two dads came riding down the rough road on their bikes, each pulling a small trailer full of gear and food. They told me that the nine kilometres from the parking area near the main road had been a rough and slow ride, but it was okay. It had taken them a couple of hours. "Hmmm, a rough, slow couple of hours on mountain bikes," I thought. "Even rougher and slower on foot I'll bet." They described a very wide deep trench located right at the start, a dry moat apparently excavated by park staff to keep motorized vehicles off the bush road and out of the area. Even walking their bikes around the trench had been tricky. The vision of leisurely driving my Toyota Corolla down to pick up my heavy gear evaporated like a little puff of smoke. A nine-kilometre grunt portage took its place.

I told them a short description of my situation, apologized for setting up camp right in front of their rented cabin, then quickly went and moved my tent 30 metres along the side of the bush road, parallel to the river, out of their way. Once they had settled into the cabin, they all came back out and invited me over to the campfire circle. The men thanked me for having already lit the fire for them, and we talked awhile. They even gave me a beer.

After some discussion, we agreed their bikes and trailers couldn't possibly haul my heavy barrel and canoe pack. Also, if I hiked out, or even biked out, without my gear in the morning, I would still, at some future time, need to walk back in to get it all, and then have to turn around and hike everything back out. No, I wouldn't do that nine-kilometre hike three times. I would take it all in one big go the next day.

I resolved to get up before first light and pack everything into the minimum number of pieces. With an early start and steady effort, I calculated I should be at the main park road in time to catch that possible noon shuttle.

Declining their further friendly offers of more conversation, food, and even another beer, I went to bed exhausted. Relishing lying flat, I finally allowed myself to begin relaxing. Through the screen door of my tent I watched the river quietly flow by. The soft pastel glow of sunset, reflected on the quiet water, reminded me again that nature is so beautiful, so wonderful, and life is so precious.

Nevertheless, my sleep was fitful again, interrupted repeatedly by worries about what I still had to do, and terrifying imaginings of being trapped beneath the surface, bubbles rising.

End of the Portage

7

An hour before any glimmer of dawn, my watch alarm went off, and I forced myself awake. The neighbours slept on in the old cabin while, holding my small flashlight, I quietly emptied and dropped my tent. After a quick breakfast and three cups of coffee, I packed everything as compactly as possible. By 4:45 the job was done. I did a careful final sweep, loaded myself, and quietly followed the curve of the bush road away from the river.

As expected, taking all my stuff in one go proved to be a real grunt, the heaviest single load I'd ever carried. When I had been packing back at home, I thought everything would be easily brought along with me in the floating canoe most of the time. There would be occasional short or medium-length portages, but on those, if necessary I would make three trips, like I had done at Crooked Chute. Since I wasn't carrying a boat with me that morning, I pondered whether "portaging" was the most accurate word to describe what I was doing, but it certainly wasn't going to be short or medium-length. All those unnecessary items I had tossed in and brought along were now just extra weight.

For the first half-hour, I walked slowly in the dark, using the beam of my little flashlight to watch for stumbling hazards. Plodding along, sometimes staggering, I kept looking at my watch, waiting for the first hint of daylight. When a faint glow finally became bright enough to make the path visible, I stopped for the first of many short rests. Already quite tired, I off-loaded everything clumsily and sat down on top of the food barrel. At least now my flashlight could be put away. But there would be no more half-hour hikes between breaks. From then on, the longest I could make it before stopping would be fifteen minutes.

At that first stop, I worked out the most efficient system for loading myself up. First, I would sit on the ground in front of the heavy, jammed-full barrel pack, and reaching back, slip my arms through the shoulder straps. My two paddles hung out behind, wedged in an X configuration through the back of the harness. The deep-dish yoke, torn from my canoe, my only memento, hung back there as well, stuffed through the middle of the X. Once I had the straps squarely on my shoulders, I had to roll carefully to one side then get onto my hands and knees, with the barrel above my back. From there, slowly and carefully, I stood up. Next came the bulky turquoise canoe pack, complete with its strapped-on tent. After lifting it slightly off the ground by its shoulder straps, I would swing it back and forth in front of me once or twice, then heave it quickly upwards and backwards while keeping hold of the straps. When I did this just right, and more than a few times I didn't, it would land with a thud just behind my head, and sit perched on top of the barrel lid. I then quickly hooked both of its padded straps over my forehead, voyageur tumpline style. My final maneuver was to bend both knees just enough so that I could reach down and grab the red teardrop pack, with its clipped-on water bottle. Straightening up again, I would steady myself for a second, then head off. I must have repeated this procedure twenty times.

My aim was to maintain a steady pace, but also to be alert. There was that ever-present lemon that comes from travelling alone. An injury would not only slow me down, it could cripple me. There would be no quick help. Probably no help at all. At the end of each short shift, exhaustion forced me to put everything down and take a break. A couple of times I toppled over sideways in the process of loading myself back up, and had to start all over. Although frustrating, this made me laugh, because it was as if I was a child's roly-poly toy. Huge relief washed through me each time I allowed myself to put everything down. My admiration for the legendary strength, speed, and stamina of the fur trade voyageurs increased steadily as I plodded along, my own pace being more like that of an old mule.

Steady breathing and the beat of my footsteps kept a rhythm going, as thoughts bounced around my head. After a while, many moments began to feel enriched, sharply focussed. Beautiful flickers of sunlight shimmered through fluttering leaves. A bird with a slight reverb in its lovely tinkling voice would call nearby. A few seconds later, a much more distant bird, with a very similar song, would reply. Now and then little puffs of breeze would stroke my face like a soft gentle hand. Looking down, I would be struck by the intricate delicate shape of an individual fern leaf, then realize there were hundreds, maybe thousands more in this community. Strange-looking insects sometimes crossed the trail, scurrying out of the way of my giant feet. The complexity of the trees, plants, birds and butterflies, the bright stained-glass windows of sky high above the canopy, even the fresh air in my lungs, all deepened my love of nature as I trudged.

My mind also mused over some philosophical concepts, especially pondering thankfulness and grace. Surely good fortune had shone on me, again and again. If I found myself starting to fixate on my aches and pains, or my poor ruined canoe, I would remind myself that there were many millions of people much less fortunate than me in this world, people who had experienced in their lives, or might even be experiencing at that very moment, terrible suffering, tragedy and pain, oceans deeper than any I had ever known.

Near the outset, just after daybreak, I had noticed there were a few fresh canine tracks on the path. Too large for a fox, they were almost certainly made by a wolf. Perhaps it had been returning from a night visit near my tent, or somewhere along the river's edge. Off and on during most of my hike, I saw those same large paw prints, always with their bent claws pointing forward, going my way. Rather than being worried about possibly catching up to this wolf, or it approaching me in some kind of menacing way, I ignored the echoes of stories and films that portray false or exaggerated frightening impressions of the natural world. No, I felt blessed to be walking in the footsteps of that wolf. "Good company!" I thought. "Why shouldn't this animal, who lives here or nearby in this forest that I am only briefly passing through, take the easiest route like me?" It probably knew the trail quite well.

The wolf was too smart to let me see anything other than its tracks. Although I watched carefully, I never caught a glimpse. But it comforted me to think of it, out there somewhere nearby, living wild and free, perhaps even watching.

Thank goodness this park and other natural spaces exist, protecting wild creatures and places that many of us can only imagine.

Forced to make so many stops, I estimated my average hiking speed was only two kilometres an hour. After four hours, I was sure I must be getting close to the main road, and started looking for the large ditch the bicycle family had described. But after five hours, there was still no trench. I was beginning to get discouraged when I glimpsed what seemed like a vision up ahead! First, I caught a twinkling flash through the forest, a glint, perhaps of shiny metal, like I had seen from the ATV. Then, as if in a dream, a very high pickup truck slowly emerged, lumbering from the foliage. It was crawling, rocking its way slowly along the rough trail, and heading right toward me! A jolt of electricity zinged through me! It was a park vehicle, a high suspension utility pickup truck.

In a couple of minutes, it rolled up right beside me. As I lowered my packs to the ground, the uniformed park warden inside stuck his head out the window and said, "Are you Phil?" Surprise, relief, thankfulness and joy shot through me. I realized my ATV friend must have made his first phone call. I was suddenly back in the world of motorized assistance. After confirming my name, I blurted out a rapid-fire two-sentence version of my story. Thanking him sincerely for his offer of a lift, I chucked my gear into the back of his truck, and hopped in front.

The incredible softness of the car seats sank in immediately. The driver told me the Algonquin Portage store had received a call from someone at 9:00 that morning. Knowing that only this super-high park vehicle would be capable of getting down this bush road, they had phoned the Achray staff base, and a short while later my welcome knight in shining fenders had driven up. I looked at my watch. It was just after

10:00. I'd been hiking since 4:45; five-and-a-quarter hours to walk nine kilometres!

The warden executed a leisurely five-point turn in some low bushes, then started the truck rolling slowly back along the path, toward the main park road. I took my last look down the trail, through the forest, toward the river, and the places gone by, then drifted back into the present, the world of soft seats, people and machines.

In only three minutes we reached the huge ditch. I had been so close! We crept down the steep incline, rolled cautiously across the wide trench, two big wheels at a time, and crawled up the other side. It felt like a monster-truck circus act. Because the body of this specialized truck was suspended so high, far above the tops of its tires, we were able to perform the trick easily. My kids would have been impressed. I certainly was.

The driver confirmed that park staff had dug this obstacle in the Crooked Chute ranger cabin bush road to make it impassable for almost any vehicle, forcing all visitors to either hike or bike in, after carefully walking around the waterless moat. He also said that these days, even park staff rarely go down the trail, usually only to do occasional maintenance on the cabin, or in difficult situations like mine.

On hearing this and seeing the demonstration of the truck's ability, I realized that if I had simply stayed sleeping in my little tent by the cabin that morning, my rescuer would have pulled up there at around 10:30 a.m. and driven me and all my gear out. I would have been spared the marathon schlep! But it was no matter. I was proud to have hiked out under my own power, through the beautiful morning forest, in the footsteps of the wolf, philosophizing.

As we drove along I told him more details. At first, he was likely sizing me up, deciding if I was just another careless rookie, someone with no proper map, or knowledge of whitewater. Maybe he eventually realized from listening, or perhaps from looking at my paddles and other gear, that I was actually a fairly experienced tripper, someone who had paddled a lot of whitewater, but this time, had made crucial mistakes.

The warden left me standing by my car in the Lac Travers parking area. I was extremely grateful for his help, but he wouldn't take any money. "Part of the job," he said. So I asked him if he knew about sweetgrass. I was happy to tell him a little of what I have learned from Mohawk and Algonquin friends. This includes the fact that sweetgrass is legal, and has been used with deep respect by Indigenous Peoples for more than 6,000 years. I told him a quote, a teaching that a Mohawk elder had said to me many years earlier: "When the smoke goes on you, the smudge, and you smell the smoke, it's a purification. It helps you speak your truth, and reminds you that everything will be alright – but not necessarily how you think." I thought of the little piece left by the Rollway fire circle. My rescuer smiled and graciously accepted the last short section of my PFD braid, along with my deep thanks. With a friendly wave out the window, he drove away. A circle was complete. There was a new braid of sweetgrass under my seat.

The drive home was a pleasure-filled experience. Such cushy softness! Such fabulous music, and speed! The lovely breeze through the widow caressed my face and hair. Driving through the park at 50 kilometres per hour, it felt as if the car was flying. I stopped on my way out at the park's Sand Lake Gate office and explained who I was. Yes, they had heard about me. I signed a few papers regarding my material losses, asking them to please let me know if anything should happen to be washed up, or be handed in sometime. Of course, nothing ever was.

I also stopped at the Algonquin Portage store and thanked them for relaying the phone call that morning. I smiled at the familiar wooden "Thank You" sign displayed up on the wall above the main store window. My school board's Outdoor Education Subject Council had given this to the owners years ago, a small token for their extensive and generous help over several years to school groups on Outdoor Education trips. They had especially helped many times with the storage of our canoes and trailers. I had brought many high school groups into the store on their way in or out of the park, often for ice cream. This time, they had helped me out personally. Outfitters and experienced trippers do understand.

As my pleasure-mobile rolled along, I thought about all the people who had helped me since the wreck: the two paddlers who ferried me upriver and loaned me money (which I did later repay); the ATV driver who offered his food and a ride, and made the phone calls (He later did call me at my home, as pre-arranged. Happily, I was safe and sound, and able to tell him how it all turned out); the two biker dads at the Crooked Chute cabin who offered me food, assistance, and beer; the warden driver, who got me to my car with my gear and dignity intact; and the Algonquin Portage store staff who relayed the call to the park. I counted seven people who had helped me out, in less than forty-eight hours. I found this wonderful, yet not surprising. Anyone who thinks people are generally selfish or unhelpful, needs only to paddle a little to have their faith restored. Most of the time, people are very good. When given the chance or the necessity, we are there for each other.

On my drive home from a trip, I often phone Jill to say hi, and let her know I'm on my way. This time I didn't. Despite my two days of trials, it turned out that I was actually returning home right on time, on the exact day I had planned to end the trip. Except of course, I had planned to return with my canoe.

I drove in the driveway and Jill came out to greet me. Smiling her wonderful welcoming smile, she asked how my trip was. When I grinned sheepishly, she glanced up at the top of the car, then back to me, then back once more to the top. She slowly twigged, looked me in the eye, tilted her head a little to the side, and said, "Um... Where... is..... your boat?" I suggested we go in and sit down, that I had quite a story to tell.

End of the Portage

PART 2

Sweet are the uses of adversity.

William Shakespeare, *As You Like It*, Act 2 Scene 1

End of the Portage

8

People who didn't know me well asked why on earth I would ever want to get back into a canoe and go out on a rushing river again. My family and friends had no need to ask. They knew I would eventually return to doing what I loved.

My goal on the August 2005 Petawawa trip, of reaching that Big Cliffs campsite, had vanished abruptly when I pinned my canoe. Moments later, as I stepped down into the river, gathered some gear, and started my slow walk through neck-deep water, that objective, and nearly every other goal I had, became irrelevant. Only two priorities remained in my life: surviving, and getting home to my loved ones. Thankfully, luck, or grace, was with me. I made it home, and got to hug my wife.

Less than two weeks later, when the immediate shock from the crisis had subsided, I was sitting comfortably at home when it came to me. There was an upside, a previously unthought-of possibility that would never have crossed my mind if it weren't for the accident. Wrecking and abandoning my canoe had surely slammed a door in my life, but it had opened another. I could start thinking about buying myself a new boat.

For a couple of days, I considered getting a good quality used boat, but quickly discarded that idea. No, a brand new canoe would be best at this point in my life. We could manage it financially, and a new canoe would last many years, hopefully decades. I had been fortunate, and able to opt for early retirement at 55. My thirty years of teaching would be complete at the end of the school year that was just about to begin. A canoe would be the perfect retirement present to give myself. Besides, when would I ever get another chance? So, as my last year of teaching started in September 2005, I allowed myself the luxury of preparing to buy a brand-new whitewater canoe.

Like my old boat, it would be a canoe where I would know its whole history, and each future scratch and dent would be from a story I might remember, or choose to forget. I promised myself I would take better care of it, and not wreck this one. My old boat had done great service for over fourteen years. Maybe someday this one might go to one of my kids.

Choosing my new canoe took almost four months. All autumn and early winter, I worked on it in my spare time. It was an enjoyable research process that involved reading, listening to the recommendations and preferences of paddler friends and sales people, and comparing models, prices, construction materials, manufacturers, and retailers. I also enjoyed just browsing around, looking at different kinds of canoes.

In the end, after weighing everything carefully, I bought the newest edition of the very same boat I had lost to the Petawawa River: the red, 16-foot (5 metre) Mad River Explorer, with its hull made of tough ABS/Royalex plastic. There were very slight modifications in the design and materials, such as the fact that they used all-capitals this time in the white logo on the side, and a slightly thinner Royalex to reduce the weight a bit. But it was essentially the same canoe. My old Mad River had always been perfect for me. It fit my uses, body size, and habits the best, so I went with my gut feeling, and bought what I knew.

In mid-January of 2006 I ordered it. A friend at the store said, with a smile, that not many people in Ottawa buy canoes in January. But I wanted to have it ready to catch the early spring runs in late March and early April. I ordered my canoe with ash gunwales and thwarts, just like my old boat. But since these have now been replaced by vinyl in most modern whitewater canoes, there wasn't a boat in stock anywhere in Canada or the Northeastern US that fit my order. Mine had to be specially made for me by the folks at the Mad River Canoe factory.

Possibly due to the request for ash gunwales, it somehow took a surprising five months before the manufacturer actually delivered my freshly minted boat in late June. Thankfully, during the long waiting period, my retailer gave me use of a free loaner, one of their own rental whitewater canoes, so I was able to get my usual fix of a couple of high-water early spring day-trips with friends. It was good to be back on the water, but I wanted to be out there in my own new canoe.

On June 21st, the Summer Solstice, ten months after my accident on the Petawawa, the manufacturer delivered. I drove home from the retail store with my pride and joy on the roof, unloaded it, went in the house, and got Jill. She carried our paddling equipment while I portaged my beautiful new red canoe 350 metres down our street to the wide, slow-moving flatwater section of the Ottawa River near our house. As the fat Midsummer sun set over the glorious mirror of the open river, we went for a short celebratory first paddle together.

The Summer Solstice is "First Nations Day" in Canada. As we travelled in the virgin boat, we kept in mind the fact that canoes are a gift and a legacy from the First Peoples. We drifted, spotlit in the reflected shimmering gold, and respectfully burned a little of the new sweetgrass braid from my PFD pocket. "Everything will be alright – but not necessarily how you think."

As the final weeks of June passed, I said goodbye to my last classes of wonderful, energetic high school students. I've always loved teaching, and knew that the saddest part of retirement for me was going to be that I would no longer have day-to-day contact with large numbers of teenagers. Sure, there were many stresses at school, but the students gave so much back, and had helped keep me current. I would miss them.

But it was time to do other things. I felt very fortunate to have the chance. There were many great elements of retirement to look forward to, including having more time and energy for being with Jill, visiting our kids, perhaps writing, playing music, painting, and of course, paddling and camping. I would be able to focus on whatever work or interests I chose, and there would be room for new directions I couldn't imagine.

After completing all my final school tasks, I went to the office and handed in the keys. As I walked down those hallways one last time, past the locked door of my classroom, I told myself it was just a place, a place that I was leaving. I walked out to the parking lot and drove away.

During those same last two weeks of June, in the evenings and on weekends, I experienced the deep satisfaction of personally custom rigging my new canoe, as it sat on its sawhorses in our yard. Besides the lovely wood gunwales, I bought it with a deep-dish ash yoke pre-installed, the same type of beautifully sculpted neck-saver I had put in my old Mad River years ago. When this kind of yoke sits on your neck on a portage, it's so comfortable that I swear it takes several kilograms off the perceived weight.

The previous summer, while standing in the rushing river beside my wreck, I had ripped my old yoke out of the boat at the last minute because it was just too good to leave. Shortly after I came home, I installed it in our very old fiberglass canoe. Jill had bought that locally-made one for us, our first owned canoe, way back in 1983 when our daughter Jody and first son Daniel were very young. "The Fiberglass," as we call her, still floats without leaks, and occasionally does service on local flatwater trips, if we have a big group and need another boat. Both wide and deep, it's always been a great family canoe, providing lots of room for kids and gear. But it had come from the factory equipped with only a simple, straight, squared piece of hardwood as its centre thwart. Those hard edges had rubbed uncomfortably on my neck for decades of portages. It was gratifying on several levels to unbolt and replace it with the salvaged, much better deep-dish one. It was also comforting to see that at least part of my old boat was still carrying on, doing good service.

To give my new Mad River extra strength, which is especially helpful in whitewater, I had also bought, and bolted in, a stern thwart. This again, was the same reinforcement I had done in my old canoe. Although the lovely smooth new gunwales, seats and thwarts had already been lightly oiled at the factory, for good measure I gave them an additional protective coating of tung oil. I planned to coat them again after the first season, using clear, hard marine varnish, for even greater protection.

Small metal D-rings were glued to the grey insides of the hull on either side of the bow and stern, as anchors for clipping in my new, big, lemon-yellow floatation airbags, front and back. I also very carefully drilled a couple of three-eighths inch holes near the top of the nose and rear of the hull, just below the small wooden decks. Wincing as I drilled through the top of the ABS, I knew this minor surgery was necessary so I could snuggly fit through, and tie, small half loops of heavy-duty blue rope. These would serve as strong, reliable grab handles for easy carrying and for tying painters, each one big enough for a hand to hold, but small enough that they would never accidentally catch a foot or an arm in an upset.

Lastly, and for everyone's present and future comfort, on the floor I glued in eight pieces of thick, grey, closed-cell foam. These would act as permanent knee-pads, two for each of the four possible paddling positions. No-one's knees would ever be chafed while paddling my boat.

I finished the outfitting job on Canada Day, July 1st, the day after I retired. I would certainly miss the students, but not for a second would I be at a loss for things to do. My new, fully rigged boat sat upside down on its sawhorses in the back yard, waiting.

To have a new canoe, and the time to use it! Such luxury! As the massive fireworks display filled Ottawa's skies near Parliament Hill, Jill and I beamed at each other.

9

Deciding where to go for our first big trip was quite an enjoyable task. There are so many wonderful wild places to choose from, and different ways to configure a trip. Jill and I eventually came up with a plan to start the summer with what, for us, was a perfect nine-day paddling holiday. First, we would share an intimate five-day lakeside camping experience together, just the two of us. Then Jill would head home and I would continue on, and do a four-day river solo.

We've become spoiled when it comes to picking our camp-site locations. Given good conditions, and if we aren't out with a group, Jill and I will nearly always choose to do paddle-in camping, or as Ontario Parks calls it, interior or back-country camping, rather than car-camping. We know that if our car is somewhere near our tent, we will also likely be set up close to other people. When living in the city, which for us is most of the time, it's understood there will always be a lot of people around us. But when we head off to camp and live outdoors for a while, we treasure our solitude. The fewer signs of others the better. All our favourite sites over the years have been in large natural spaces, with no, or few, other campers nearby.

The primary aim of our paddling trips is to distance ourselves for a while from the human-centred world, and connect intimately with nature. We usually keep to ourselves out there, except for being with family or friends if they're along. Occasionally we enjoy chatting with the few people we encounter, and often they are wonderful. But most of the time we prefer being on our own. There will be plenty of time for socializing back in town.

Nature's own sound levels soon become our normal. Ideally, almost every sound that isn't made by us, will be made by birds, animals, wind or water. Our own noises, such as rattled pots, accidental bumps on a boat, or talking, tend to become softer and less frequent the longer we camp.

Immersion in nature is so restorative and precious. Unlike false representations sometimes portrayed in fiction, natural areas are places to approach with respect and preparation, not fear. Our many paddling and camping experiences have given us countless marvelous positive memories. These in turn have had lasting effects on our values, and those of our children.

My own memories of times in natural spaces were fundamental in developing and supporting a long-term core goal of mine throughout my teaching years. This was to help as many people as possible to have great educational experiences outside in nature. Via various Outdoor Education formats, I tried to help students of all ages to know, understand, and love the natural world and their place in it – especially those who might otherwise not have had an opportunity to get out there. I've personally benefited immeasurably from my many times in nature. How could I not want to pass it on?

For years, the favourite location for Jill and I to go for a paddle-in flatwater camping trip has been in the heart of Algonquin Park at Lake Travers. I've heard the word Travers pronounced several ways, but we simply say it as if it is the same word with an "e" on the end: "traverse" – which means to cross. We don't worry if it is correct or not. Our family has spent many happy days and nights on that big, clean Canadian Shield lake, camping, paddling, swimming and hiking. Although our three kids are all now adults and living far away, Jill and I still enjoy camping there.

Travers has excellent individual campsites around its rim, but not too many. They're spread out and secluded, the way we like it. Best of all, you have to go by boat to get to any of them. A few have sand beaches, some have large Shield rocks, and several are lined with shallow cobblestone shores where, in mid- to late- summer, stands of crimson cardinal flowers welcome paddlers to their temporary home.

The surrounding rolling hills, are covered with pine, cedar, balsam, hemlock, maple, birch, beech and oak. Though logged many years ago, the forest has grown up again and looks natural and mature. There are also a few large marshes where hawks, osprey, or rarely, an eagle might be seen. Ravens can often be heard croaking back and forth across the sky. Soft peeps and chips from wee flitting chickadees and sparrows enliven the low bushes near the water. Years ago, we used to occasionally hear the romantic sound of a train in the distance, but the line through the park has long since been decommissioned and turned into a walking trail.

Loons love this lake, and are a favourite of ours. We know they will always be part of any trip to Lake Travers. Although often quiet during daylight hours, a camper can usually count on hearing their calls, either at dusk, or perhaps during the deepest, darkest part of the night. This iconic sound confirms that we are indeed sleeping in the Canadian wild. Sounding eerie and otherworldly, a loon might sometimes be heard cooing like a moaning ghost, softly, almost imperceptibly, far in the distance down the lake. At other times, we may enjoy hearing a pair do a musical call-and-response conversation far out on the water. Sometimes one will fly directly over our camp, its loud, shrill repeating tremolo sounding like a hysterical laugh. During the day, a loon might be seen far out on the lake doing a splendid dance, almost standing on the water, as it displays the white undersides of its open, flapping wings. A lucky paddler might even get to see one of these big birds up close, but perhaps not for long. A loon, which one minute is almost right beside the boat, will often slip silently under the water and disappear. The observer is left waiting, scanning in every direction, until a few minutes later, the bird finally surfaces a long way off.

Because Jill and I have so many positive memories of camping there, Lake Travers was our obvious pick to start off the summer. Jill would paddle her trusty red 12-year-old River Runner R5 Excel kayak, and I my brand new canoe. For five days and nights, we planned to relax and enjoy full summer on the lake. There would be plenty of time for shaking off residual tensions from the end of the school year, and for enjoying each other's company. Our not-so-busy itinerary would involve day-tripping, hiking, swimming, reading, and lots of lying in the hammock. That would be Part One.

On our sixth day out, Part Two would start. After taking down and packing up our Lake Travers camp, we would load our boats and paddle back across the lake to the car. Several items would be dropped off, plus I would pick up some others from the trunk. There would be re-sorting and a considerable downsizing of the contents of my canoe. Then I would load Jill's kayak onto the roof racks, and we would say goodbye. She would drive home with most of our comfort-camping stuff, while I continued on alone, carrying a considerably reduced load. I would paddle all the way to the very far end of Lake Travers, then head down the Petawawa.

Yes, I would go back. Back to complete the four-day journey I couldn't finish the previous summer. Back to do it right. This would include returning to the scene of my wreck. However, unlike last year's harsh trip ending, this time my plan was to sleep at the same little Rollway campsite, then portage everything in the morning, and paddle on. I would make it to that Big Cliffs campsite this time, then continue all the way to McManus Lake. That would be Part Two.

Jill and I are blessed in so many ways, including that we have the shared interests, resources, experience, and time to do this sort of complex tripping holiday. A two-part expedition has a lot of logistics to sort out. Working through the organizational puzzle is like solving a mystery in reverse. And of course, as with any good mystery, it's all in the set-up. Forget something, and it can really affect your experience. For our first big trip with the new canoe, we wanted everything to work out perfectly. This was especially true for me on my solo time.

We would use our two Toyota Corollas to drive to Algonquin, and drop one off at the parking area for McManus Lake on our way to Travers. This was so that, after our five days together, Jill would be able to drive home, while I paddled the river. The waiting car would allow me to do my own easy shuttle home at the end of my solo.

In the trunk of the McManus car, a set of four rooftop canoe sponges would be left, and several ropes to tie the canoe on top when I arrived. Since this was going to be my end-of-the-trip vehicle, it didn't need to have a lot of other supplies left inside: just a can of juice, a couple of granola bars, and a set of clean clothes, including a pair of dry shoes, just in case.

Meanwhile the other car, our Lake Travers vehicle, would be stuffed full, carrying everything else for all nine days.

When the morning of the start of our adventure came, I installed my heavy-duty metal roof racks on the Lake Travers car, ready to carry both Jill's kayak plus the new Mad River to the lake, upside down, side by side. The paddles were tied inside the canoe to save space. The trunk and body of the car carried our 4-person tent (perfect for two plus gear) for our time together on Lake Travers, and my little 2-person tent (perfect for one plus gear) for my solo. The food for my river trip was preloaded in its own big blue barrel, which would remain in the car while we were out camping together on the lake. All the food for Jill and I during our five days together was in a second large blue barrel that would come with us. The rest of our sleeping and camping gear was also packed into the very full Travers car, along with our comfort supplies, such as Jill's hammock, my big folding chair, art materials, and books. Careful clothing selections had been made, with care not to overdo it. Mine were all packed in my big waterproof turquoise canoe pack.

With preparations complete, we drove away in our two-car convoy on Tuesday, July 4th, the day after the Canada Day long weekend. This is my favourite time on any trip, when the prep work is all done, the boats are ready and up on top, the gear and food are in, and the adventure is just beginning. As we drove toward the park, the weather was perfect: a bright, hot, sunny summer day, with a cloudless blue sky.

After dropping off the McManus car, we continued roughly 50 kilometres deeper into the park, to the parking lot at the interior access point for Lake Travers. With the holiday weekend finished, there were hardly any vehicles parked there. Excellent! We backed right up to the put-in and, with our usual stellar teamwork, unloaded the car and readied our two-boat fleet in twenty minutes.

As always when canoeing alone, I would be paddling my Mad River in the solo position, in other words, sitting on or kneeling in front of the bow seat, facing the stern. Jill's kayak has only a small cargo hatch, so it would just carry a few items. We crammed everything else into the canoe. By the time it was fully loaded, ready to head off, my sleek whitewater boat had been transformed into a heavily laden freighter. I drove the car to a shady spot in the parking area, did a quick final check in case we had forgotten anything, and locked it. Feeling fantastic, I walked back to Jill and the boats.

The put-in for Lake Travers is at the lower end of a section of the Petawawa River called Poplar Rapids. It's near the place where the river flows into the southwestern end of the big lake. The lake itself is a long, broad widening of the Petawawa. Ten kilometres to the northeast, at the farthest end of the lake, where the waters narrow and become a river again, the Petawawa flows back out, at Big Thompson Rapids.

The moving water pouring past the put-in from the bottom of Poplar Rapids, means that boaters returning from the lake to their vehicles must paddle against a medium current for a couple of minutes. But this is usually not difficult. That same little push from the Petawawa also gives a helpful downriver send-off to all paddlers as they start their journeys. We burned a little sweetgrass and pushed off.

End of the Portage

10

Wilderness is like a well...
For our souls.

We drink from it when we can
And even when we can't
The well is still there
For our spirits to fly to
...At any time.

An award-winning video that friends and I made about our memorable 1991 Mountain River canoe trip, starts and ends with this message slowly scrolling up the screen. Although I wrote the words so long ago, when Jill and I emerged from the Petawawa mouth and started across Lake Travers, I thought of them again and smiled. We were about to have a good long drink.

Seeing us out there together, paddling our red boats once more on the serene lake, under the giant blue sky, filled me with a familiar deep joy. I wished I could somehow capture the scene with paint on a huge canvas, or maybe take the perfect photograph. I settled for engraving it in my memory.

After crossing about a quarter of the lake, Jill went ahead in her speedy kayak to find us a good campsite. She soon gave me the paddles-up signal to come along, while she waited just offshore. The large site she found has long been one of our favourites, and we were happy to see it unoccupied. It's nestled in a level grove of reforested red pine, and among its special features there is a lovely sand beach, almost half a kilo-metre long.

Ten minutes later, the nose of my freighter slid onto the beach. I clambered carefully on hands and knees across the mound of gear, until I could step out onto dry sand. Jill then brought her kayak in beside me and I helped her get out. It didn't take long for us to unload everything and carry it up the little rise to the tent and fire-circle area. After picking up a few small leftover bits of litter, we went about setting up our base-camp.

Then for five glorious days and nights we relaxed, day-tripped, swam, walked the beach, went for hikes, and enjoyed a lovely, easy camp life. Full summer smiled on us every single day with perfect, sunny, warm weather. Cerulean blue skies floated only small puffy white clouds, without any hint of rain. We had no strong winds, and the occasional breezes, when they came, were light and welcome. As a wonderful bonus, there were hardly any bugs. We had brought our bug jackets with us, but never needed to wear them. Each night the sky was either partly or completely clear, showcasing an ocean of stars. The well steadily filled us.

It felt so comfortable, and so right to be there, just the two of us. Camping trips with friends or school groups can be great times, and usually involve a lot of memorable fun and comradery. But this was a different kind of experience. There's nothing like spending a little time camping one-to-one with the person you love.

As with most trips in the outdoors, successive days got better and better. In a yoga class they might call this "relaxing into the pose." There's a calming of the spirit. Senses become more finely tuned. With nothing to prove or defend, and no firm schedule, inner peace comes easily.

On a one-to-one trip like this, Jill and I become more sensitive to each other, and also to the natural world. The wonders of nature completely surround us. It's so much easier to know that we are part of everything when out in the wild, than it is in the city. Paraphrasing the words of Henry David Thoreau in *Walden*, when we camp, we listen to a different drummer.

There's plenty of time for thoughts to be casually sifted, sorted, discarded or treasured. There's time to start again, or maybe end something; time for healing; time to reshuffle or rewrite priorities. Then again, one or both of us might simply sit and watch the lake for an hour or two, walk the sand, or maybe go for a dip. I find that my nose takes increased notice of the pleasant natural smells, such as the delicate aroma of the soft pine needles that blanket large areas from the many white and red pine trees. After a lovely lake swim, our feet first feel the sand, then the silky carpet of pine needles, and sometimes the sponginess of a thick clump of moss.

A long, gentle arc of undisturbed beach curves from the campsite, far down to the left, past some low sand cliffs. Along the way, the narrow dark brown lining, the water's edge, is refreshingly cool. Since we had such consistently great weather, the dry sand further from the water often felt burning hot by mid-afternoon, sometimes making us do funny tip-toe dances on our way to the water. Long after dark, the big smooth beach boulders were still warm to the touch, and made great perches for star gazing, sitting and thinking, or just sitting.

Life became simplified. If we got warm, we swam. If we got cold, we added layers. If we got restless, we paddled or hiked. If we felt tired, we sat or lay down. We chatted about whatever was on our minds. Sometimes we sorted through issues, or made plans. We got closer.

Many times each day I would gaze at the sky, either whimsically pondering its beauty or looking for tell-tale signs of a weather change. Sometimes I would take a relaxed half hour to slowly prepare an afternoon cup of tea for Jill, served in the hammock, occasionally with a special side dish treat, such as peeled sections of a fresh orange, reminiscent of the Leonard Cohen song *Suzanne*. If we made a small supper fire, there was always plenty of time afterward to sit quietly and enjoy its crackle and hiss, and the sweet pungent smell of pine woodsmoke.

Whenever we pleased, we would read, write, sketch or have a nap. Often we would chat about aspects of the natural environment, or exclaim to each other how fabulous it was to be there. So many people would love to have the opportunity to do this. We knew we were blessed.

Once or twice a day, we would hear a distant motor hum from a low-powered aluminum boat. Following the trail of sound with our eyes, we might see heat-shimmering silhouettes of a fishermen or two. Now and then, further out, near the centre of the lake, there would be a canoe or two moving slowly along. Occasionally we saw large groups of eight or nine boats, probably heading for Big Thompson and the Petawawa. Rarely, we would look way up high, and spy a tiny silver jet, heading west. There was no sound.

In the middle of one of our calmest and clearest nights, I gently woke Jill. We crawled out of the tent, and put our PFDs on over top of our night clothes. The canoe was readied quietly, and we got in and slipped away from shore. Floating silently like a spaceship on the mirror surface, we were thrilled and inspired by the millions of stars above, and their twinkling reflections on the water. We watched a few tiny satellites speed along way up there, and a couple of times were surprised and elated by the fireworks of shooting stars, blazing brief lines. Again there was no sound. Even the lake's normal gentle lapping against the shore was stilled on this night. We could hear each drip from the paddle and, when we listened closely, our own breathing. Concepts like infinity, and the vastness of the universe, became undeniable realities. Our spirits filled to overflowing.

After as much awe as we could handle for one night, I slipped my paddle back in and, as quietly as I could, floated us slowly back to the beach. With stars shining below in the water, and above in the heavens, we glided in, as if docking with the mother space station. There was a very small bump as the nose skidded softly onto the sand. Back to base. We stepped ashore, still staring all around in amazement. I slid the canoe up onto the dry sand, and turned it upside down for the night. We crawled back in the tent, snuggled into our sleeping bags, and went back to sleep, closer, richer, happier. Life was very good.

Most days began with me getting up early, before Jill, and making us coffee. Jill claims that my "Phil's First Run Camp-Coffee," is much better than the coffee in any coffee shop chain. There are likely as many ways to make camp-coffee as there are campers, and I can't claim to have invented my preferred technique. With personal modifications, it's a method that was passed along to me by other tripper friends a long way down the line.

Jill would usually still be sleeping while I did this procedure, and I would wake her gently by bringing her two cups, fixed with whitener and her sweetener, the way she likes it. After the first taste, she would often enthusiastically exclaim that I must go into business selling it. Of course, it would be kind of hard to replicate the woodsy ambiance.

As with opinions about how to make coffee, philosophy, religion, politics, how to set up a tarp, or how to train a dog, when it comes to food on camping trips, everyone has their own ideas. Some people shop and prepare food for weeks before a trip, and take hours at their campsite cooking each gourmet meal. That's fine for them. My own thinking is that camp food should be simple and easy, fast to prepare, filling, eaten without much fuss, and require only a short clean-up. For Jill and I, this usually only takes about thirty minutes for a complete meal.

After enjoying our morning coffee, breakfast was usually simple, such as instant oatmeal packages. Most lunches were no-cook. Staples for suppers were what I like to call "food-in-a-bag," meaning a variety of purchased, excellent quality, gourmet, dehydrated food meals, prepared in their own pouch in ten minutes by simply stirring in a couple of cups of boiling water. Rounding out our menu, were apples and oranges, dried fruit, raisins, gorp (trail mix), plus granola bars and some candies. A few times we would mix things up a bit with more variety, such as hard boiled eggs, or treats such as pretzels or cookies. But our mantra was always the same: simple, easy, fast, filling, minimal fuss, short clean-up.

As is probably true for most couples and individuals when camping on their own, we get a lot of pleasure out of just doing food our own way. Our method leaves us lots of time for more pleasurable activities.

During our five days on the lake, Jill and I happily stepped off the wheel of our busy everyday lives. There were none of the usual tasks, duties, and obligations that fill our days and nights in the city. We didn't even have to deal with unpleasant weather. No, this was true free time, an extended time-out, to simply do as we pleased.

Often one or both of us would go on a paddling or hiking expedition to explore various parts of the lake. One day Jill went off in her kayak and returned a couple of hours later, stiff and achy, but with a huge smile. She had circumnavigated a nearby big island, and on the far side of it had spent an enchanted half-hour watching a mother moose with her calf, feeding in the shallows. The next day I returned to camp with my own story. Two bald eagles, rare in Algonquin in midsummer, had soared upwards in spirals directly above my canoe, until finally disappearing way up high.

Another afternoon we paddled our boats to a remote section of the lake, secured them, then hiked slowly uphill, just to see what we might find. We moved unhurriedly through the bush for half and hour, taking our time, appreciating the surroundings. It wasn't an aerobics exercise, more like wandering upwards through a tilted art gallery. We loved the fact that there were no human trails. The forest was still. We paused several times to rest and take in little sounds, the lightly scented air, and the complexity and entanglement of so many things, both living and dead.

Eventually we were rewarded by discovering a natural lookout, perched high above the lake. We wondered how long it might have been since any other person had enjoyed that splendid view. On a couple of friendly boulders, we sat and enjoyed the panorama as we ate our simple lunch. Eventually, and I don't even remember how much time had passed, we hiked slowly back down to the boats, paddled across to our camp, and had a swim and supper. What a perfect camping-trip day.

Other than a few "big" outings like these, we spent most of our days relaxing in or near base-camp. I often refer to this as "recharge time." There were many chats, but also frequent silences when neither of us felt the need to talk. Some of these stretched into solitary hours. Either close to each other, or often out of range of sight and sound, we would just do something on our own, the way young children do parallel play. Now and then, such as to have tea, a snack or a meal, we would come back together, then perhaps go off alone again. As the days passed, and our camp tasks were done more efficiently, there were even more times when things were unfocussed, times to daydream without feeling guilty, to simply sit, or wander, or mentally drift. Mainly, these were extended periods of calm and of feeling good.

Because we spent nearly all of the time out of the tent, both of us experienced many serendipitous treats from nature. A memorable one happened to me during one of those daydreaming times, as I wandered barefoot down the beach. I'd been enjoying the feeling of the perfect sand temperature on my feet, along the wet-edge. Suddenly I became aware of something large and dark moving slowly in the shallows, a few steps ahead. Feeling a bolt of primal fear, I froze.

This quickly changed to delight when I realized that what I was seeing was a huge snapping turtle. This old grandmother or grandfather was heading toward land, from somewhere out in deep water. I had spotted it under the water, about a metre from shore. As I watched, it plodded along the bottom toward the beach. When it reached the wet-edge, its raised its fist-sized dinosaur head and the front of its shell out of the water. After resting a few seconds, it began pulling and pushing with its thick legs and long claws, moving in slow motion, until it had brought itself half-way onto the sand. Once there, it stopped and rested again, this time for a couple of minutes. The old visitor then closed its eyes and seemed to go to sleep.

This was the largest snapper I'd ever seen. The low, domed top shell was longer than my forearm and wrist combined, and there was a slight peak in it above the head and neck. Its wide legs, neck, and head seemed almost too big for the shell, as if the turtle's body had outgrown it. Contributing to its ancient look, there were scraggly patches of fuzzy green algae growing on its shell. I was pretty sure this lake resident was older than me.

It was one of those moments when having a camera would have been useful, but mine was in the tent. Remaining still as a statue, I tried to etch the scene into my memory. After five minutes or so, without moving its feet or shell, the snapper blinked open its two very old-looking, and very odd-looking, eyes and turned its head slowly to the left, in my direction. It stopped when it was looking directly at me. I found myself being stared down by this amazing old-timer. Telepathically I tried to say hello.

Seeing this unexpected lake resident reminded me that I was only the most recent visitor. Like all the others, relatively speaking, I was just passing through. This turtle lived here, and had almost certainly been in this lake all of its long life. I felt honoured to see her or him. I waited for the big head to turn slowly back and look ahead, and when it shut those strange eyes again, quietly backed away. Rushing to camp, I found Jill and brought her right back to see it, but the turtle was already gone.

It may have come ashore to check out the beach as a location to lay and bury its eggs on the high sand, and so might return sometime later. For all I knew, that turtle may itself have hatched from an egg on this very beach, perhaps years before I was born. I've heard snappers can live 70 years or more. Or it could have simply come up for a little rest, to bask a while on the warm sand. Maybe it had seen me walking along, and was curious. I'll never know. But it certainly got me thinking. We know so little about the countless amazing creatures that are everywhere in the natural world. There is so much to respect, and to learn from them, and a universal need to increase the protection of their homes. I never saw the old turtle again. Perhaps it's still out there.

Although there was, of course, never any rational need to worry, since turtles will always just swim away if a person comes near, I confess that after that experience, an irrational but ingrained primal fear would sometimes make me rush out of the lake just a little bit quicker than before, when out there skinny dipping.

For many years, a major element of our camping trips has been "hammock time." This is especially true for Jill who swears by our hammock as a wonderful, and almost instantly effective, short term remedy for back pain. It's also ideal for simply relaxing, reading, taking in the view, daydreaming, or napping. We have a lovely big "two-person" hammock, made of strong, lightweight, quick-drying, silky nylon that resembles the material in a parachute. When a person lies inside, it's as if they're in a soft cocoon. We joke that we could probably easily sell this type of hammock wherever we travel, because we are such outspoken advocates.

The hammock is one of Jill's most favourite cozy places to be. She'll often go to sleep just ten minutes after climbing in. We bring it on every camping trip, hike or vacation, and always find great places with convenient trees to hang it. Having the hammock with us enables Jill or I to take a break part way along, and therefore virtually doubles the distance we can hike.

I've often teased Jill that she should write a book, complete with photographs, called, *"Jill's Favourite Hammock Spots."* There could be a chapter for each of our many favourite locations. That campsite on Lake Travers would certainly rate one.

Besides the lake area itself being a great place to camp and explore, it was never very far from my mind that this was also where my four-day solo river trip would soon start. The Petawawa was calling me. I quietly thought through strategies to make doubly sure everything went smoothly, ways to ensure my safety, plus the safety of the new boat. I swore to myself that I would avoid making critical errors this time.

The day before we left our home-away-from-home, two friendly Algonquin Park wardens were going around the lake in a small aluminum power boat, checking camping permits and the condition of the sites. Jill and I were happy to see them doing this, since they were helping ensure the ongoing protection of the park. We welcomed them to our site and the four of us had a nice chat, standing around our little campfire. After restraining myself for several minutes, I sheepishly asked the question that had been on my mind since they first pulled their boat in. Had either of them been down the Petawawa, past Rollway Rapids yet this season? I was wondering if they might have seen, or heard something about, any signs of a wrecked red canoe there, either this year, or near the end of last season? As I waited a moment for their answer, I already knew inside that all traces of my old Mad River must surely be long gone. But I had to ask. They said they hadn't been down the river themselves. But no, they hadn't heard anything from other park staff. There had been no mention of a wrecked boat. It was no surprise. I just needed to hear it.

I then told them some of the key points of my story from the previous summer. Being wardens in Algonquin Park, they must hear a lot of wild stories. They politely listened to mine, and demonstrated considerable understanding.

Just before they left, I proudly showed them my new canoe, the updated, beautiful unscratched edition of my lost one. As they got into their boat to leave, they wished me good luck on this year's solo trip. Then one of them flashed me a sly grin, and said he hoped they wouldn't need to be seeing me again.

After our five idyllic days, it was with mixed feelings that we packed everything up on the morning of day six. It was another lovely, sunny summer day. Both of us knew we would return to the lake in the future, but this particular trip had been perfect. We had been so close in every way. The grace of Mother Nature, combined with our preparation, had given us countless gifts. But it was time to go.

We loaded the boats, did a last sweep around to no-trace-the-place, and make sure nothing was left behind, and got in. Pushing off, we paddled back to the put-in quietly, slowly, side by side. There was no need to say much.

After paddling up that little push coming from the bottom of Poplar Rapids, we nosed ashore at the put-in. Back to base. I helped Jill out of her boat, and we gave each other our customary end-of-the-the-trip hearty "paddlers' handshakes," and hugs and kisses. Another circle was complete. I walked to the parking area and drove the car slowly to a few metres from the water's edge and our partially pulled-up boats. Out of the trunk, I took the preloaded second food barrel, ready for my solo, and stood it beside my canoe. Part Two was beginning.

Since we had taken our time, the hot mid-day sun was blazing as we once again demonstrated great teamwork. Most things were loaded straight into the car. Staying with me would be the bailer and spare paddle that I had brought with us on the lake, plus a second bailer, just in case. A few items were re-sorted, then everything was consolidated into either my big canoe pack, the barrel, or my small red daypack. A yellow hard-shell pelican case would carry my new camera and wallet. It, and my water bottle, would be clipped with a carabiner to the centre yoke, in easy reach. No longer a heavily laden freighter, the boat was transformed back into a fully rigged whitewater canoe, carrying a considerably lighter and trimmer load.

While Jill waited in the car, I tied her kayak securely to the roof racks. Dripping with sweat by the time I finished, I climbed into the softness of the car to sit with her for a few minutes. Jill and I have been together, as lovers and best friends, for a very long time, longer than almost any couple we know. In a month, we would celebrate 34 years of being married, plus we had been together for three years before that. In those last few minutes, sitting beside each other in the car, there was again very little need to talk. We each knew what the other was thinking and feeling.

I repeated my promises: to be extra careful, to keep safe, to return home with my boat this time. She made hers back to me: to try not to worry too much, to drive safely, and to leave the kayak on top of the car at home until I returned, so I could lift it off for her. We kissed and did a long hug. Pulling away a bit to look each other squarely in the eyes, we made forced smiles. I said, "See you soon," and got out.

For ten more minutes, she waited while I did my last fiddling with the arrangement of the gear in the canoe. I put on my PFD, did the zipper up, tied and double-checked its drawstring, then lifted the end of the canoe with its blue grab handle, so the far end floated out a little further into the water. It was time. I walked back and stood beside the car window. Smiling, we blew kisses and waved goodbye.

After the car had rolled out of sight, I did a final sweep, and walked over to the canoe. Picking up my trusty guide's paddle, I lifted the boat once more by its blue grab handle, this time sliding it out further, until it was almost completely free-floating. I stepped in carefully with one foot, bent my body forward, and keeping low, gently pushed off with the other. Quickly settling into my usual kneeling position, I started paddling.

It was eleven months since my previous solo. My watch said 4:00, but the late start wasn't anything to worry about because the weather conditions were ideal, and it wouldn't get dark until around 9:00. By that time, I would be all set up at my first campsite. The outwash from Poplar Rapids gave its friendly little send-off boost, and I was on my way.

11

In truth, although I had kept it hidden from Jill, at the very start I was a little shaky. In those last few minutes before she drove away, while adjusting the gear in the boat, my confidence had secretly wavered. For a moment, I even considered asking her to wait, so I could go home with her. Fortunately, just as suddenly, my courage and resolve returned. There was no denying it: I was compelled to go. There were very few risk lemons. As I finished arranging everything, the positive side of my brain won out, and assured the nervous side that I had surely learned from previous mistakes. I wouldn't allow fear to kill my dreams.

As I started away from the outflow of Poplar Rapids toward the open river mouth, it might have been that little boost, or maybe it was the stunning beauty of the natural world, that gave me additional positive counselling. Perhaps some kind of spirit was at work that I don't understand. Whatever it was, I felt my confidence grow increasingly stronger as I paddled. I knew that if I didn't do it this time, I would only turn around and want to do it in two weeks, a month, or in five years. It was time to take another deep drink from the well.

With a light breeze helping from behind, I emerged from the mouth of the Petawawa onto the big lake. The panorama opened wide before me, and I again felt blessed to be there. How many people would love to have this kind of opportunity! Resting my paddle across the canoe for a few minutes, I pulled out from my PFD pocket the plastic bag containing the sweetgrass braid and a lighter. I respectfully lit it, and watched it burn a bit, then let the flame go out so it would smoulder. The familiar sweet smoke washed over me, and I thought of the teachings. After a few minutes, I put my paddle back in.

As far as I could see, other than the natural inhabitants, I had the entire lake and forest to myself. My goal was to paddle the full ten kilometres of the lake, and arrive at Big Thompson Rapids very late in the afternoon. I would portage everything, paddle a short way further, then set up my first camp at the same small site I used last year, on river-left, above the start of Little Thompson. On other trips, I had enjoyed fun runs through both of these rapids, but on this trip, I would be taking extra precautions, including doing more portaging.

During the long flatwater paddle along the lake, I settled into a pleasant meditation. Things felt in balance. Life was good. There was the sky above, the water below, and me in my boat just gliding along, suspended where they meet.

As the lake eventually began its gradually narrowing, the tailwind increased and started lifting low swells. Fortunately, by going around the first bend, most of the wind was blocked and the water flattened out. During the next couple of kilometres, the lake transformed to become a wide section of the Petawawa River. It's hard to tell the exact point where the lake turns back into a river, but as the shores narrowed in closer towards each other, I watched for the first signs of a current. When the water became shallow enough that I could see that the long grass growing up from the bottom was leaning away from me, I knew I was almost back.

Half a kilometre before the Big Thompson rapids started, the low-frequency rumble could be heard in the distance. I rested my paddle across the gunwales for a minute to listen. As I floated closer, the volume increased, until it suddenly doubled as I rounded a corner and they came into sight. Often, when I hear that sound near the brink of a set of rapids, and start seeing those familiar white horses popping up and down just ahead, a strange inner sensation happens. I begin to hear a certain piece of music in my mind. It's a repetitive mantra. The music begins softly, like the sound of the rapids, and gets louder as the start of the run gets closer. It doesn't surprise me any more that, time after time, as my canoe approaches the brink, I hear "the music."

And what is this Sirens' song? It's always the same: the opening title track from the movie "Waterwalker,"[3] Bill Mason's fabulous definitive solo canoe trip feature film. Looking downriver just before floating over the point of no return, a whitewater paddler sees the river accelerate and become animated, dropping fast in elevation, as the water begins to rush, splash and dance. When I start to position my boat to paddle a rapid, that hypnotic musical riff and beat of Bruce Cockburn and Hugh Marsh's great song plays over and over in my mind. Mason and those musicians really nailed it: the anticipation, the steady strong heartbeat, and the thrill and intense pleasure of the run. Although I know the words, I usually don't hear any lyrics, only the repetitive, trance-like music. When I paddle with others, I'm surprised they don't hear it.

---

3 *Waterwalker*, Director Bill Mason, NFB, IMAGO, Creswin Films, 1984, Film, 87 minutes DVD available at   https://redcanoes. ecwid.com/DVD-4003-Waterwalker-p80193062

Mentally turning things down a little, I reminded myself that I wasn't going to run it this time. I stepped out at the head of the portage at 6:15. Walking a short way down along the shoreline, I stood on a big Canadian Shield boulder and just watched the flow. Holding the grip of my Kevlar-tipped paddle upright beside me for balance, I stared at the river's roaring power and beauty. Although excited to be there, for a fleeting moment I had a couple more nervous thoughts. Like a car crash survivor, who is back behind the wheel, and facing the on-ramp to the high-speed highway again for the first time, I solemnly asked myself, "Can I still do this?" Fortunately, the answer came back quickly: "Of course I can!"

Although there had been no rain during the five perfect days when Jill and I were on the lake, there had been a lot of rain during the spring and early summer. This meant that, unlike the previous year, the water level before me was still at the medium level, considerably higher than average for mid-summer. The run looked so easy, so tempting, so wild. The music started to play. But I kept my resolve.

Although I knew I would portage everything, nevertheless, being addicted I scouted the full length of the rapids anyway, walking all the way down the shore and back up again, for future reference. I took a few pictures with my digital camera, and made some mental notes.

The previous year, on that dry August day, when the water had been so much lower, navigating Big Thompson had looked challenging. Most of the large rocks in the river were exposed to the air. Yet, after wisely portaging my gear in two trips that time, I had successfully floated the empty old canoe through the single remaining safe channel. Of course, that was on the same trip when, the next day, I got sloppy, didn't portage my gear on Rollway, and paid for it. No, I would keep my vow to take extra precautions this time. Hopefully on some future trip, with the safety of friends along, and a positive experience from the present trip under my belt, I would run Big Thompson again.

To make doubly sure I stuck to my plan, I even took the gear out, and left it all sitting at the trailhead, while I portaged the boat first. That way I didn't have a chance to weaken and reconsider during my walk back for the second load. The music would have to wait for another journey, or more accurately, until the next day.

Just before lifting the canoe over my head, I remembered I hadn't yet given a gift to the river on this trip. In my opinion this simple custom, like many others, is well worth following. Besides any supernatural value it may or may not have, it reminds us to be respectful of the river, of where we are and what we are doing, and of those who have gone before us and those who will follow. Being respectful is so important, yet too often we forget or ignore this. The most fitting thing I could quickly find to give to the river was a shiny new quarter from my PFD pocket. I gave it a little kiss and tossed it as far upstream as I could, back toward the places gone by. After watching it twinkle and quickly disappear in the deep, I turned, picked up my canoe, and walked down the trail.

As I strolled along carrying the boat, my gift-giving reminded me of a happy memory from one of my other trips. I laughed, remembering. Many years back, during an earlier solo journey down the Petawawa in May, while camped at that favourite big Natch Cliffs campsite, I had found a large bone. It looked like a section of a moose's spine, a big piece of vertebra. I brought it home as a souvenir and kept it as a memento on my desk at the MacSkimming Outdoor Education Centre, where I was a teacher at the time.

Later, a friend pointed out that perhaps it would have been more respectful if I had left it in the river. Although not a big concern to me, over time the thought resonated. So, on a return tandem trip the following year, this time with my son Daniel and a couple of friends, I brought the bone back with me.

Shortly after we pushed off from the Lake Travers put-in at the start of that second trip, I took the bone out of my daypack and tossed it into the water at the bottom of Poplar Rapids, returning it, as a gift to the river. At that point, my friend Marc who always has a marvellous dry sense of humour, exclaimed loudly from his canoe, "Oh what was I *thinking*? I didn't bring a piece of moose spine! Now my boat is *really* in trouble!" This brought huge laughs from all of us. But nevertheless the respect was there.

As I set my new canoe down at the end of the Big Thompson portage, ready to go back for my gear, it crossed my mind that I had forgotten to give the river a gift on the previous year's trip.

Less than half an hour later I was at my first campsite, high beside Little Thompson Rapids. In the morning, I would not run this set either, and so, since the portage trail passes directly through the small campsite, I carried the canoe and all my gear up. By 7:30 I was all set for the night, and had a small supper fire lit. I thought of how Jill would probably just be getting home.

Half an hour later, I watched as four canoes paddled in from the bottom of Big Thompson to the take-out point at the base of my campsite's portage. Since the trail went right between my tent and the campfire, I had some brief company. I first chatted a bit with the two twenty-something men, who were obviously some sort of camp leaders.

Before they arrived, along with the normal dimming of the daylight, I had noticed the weather beginning to change. After six fair days, the early evening air quickly became still and muggy. Along with the constant white noise of Little Thompson, other ominous sounds began: deeper rumbles, far off, of thunder.

I cautioned the leaders, and invited them and their group to stay and camp near me. But they wanted to press on and find their own site. It's understandable, in such a large park with so much beautiful, open, wild space, and so many great campsites, to not want to be right on top of another party's camp. I feel the same way, unless it compromises safety. As the thunder grew nearer, we hurriedly looked over the Canoe Routes map and talked about other campsites coming up. I repeated my offer, but nevertheless, with ever louder booms drawing closer, but no lightning just yet, the group made a run for it.

First the leaders portaged their own packs on the double, leaving them at the put-in beside a quiet pool on river-left, beyond my site, a short distance after the big drop. They then paddled their empty canoe expertly through the deep V and rolling waves of Little Thompson. Seeing these experienced paddlers do the run with ease, I was again tempted. The six teenagers they were leading watched the show while standing with me at the high viewpoint beside my site.

The men then paddled back over to the put-in, collected their packs, and directed the others to portage all the remaining gear and their three boats to that point, as quickly as possible, via my wee camp. They did this with impressive speed and cooperation, and the four boats sped off together downriver, only thirty minutes ahead of the breaking thunderstorm.

As I gobbled my food-in-a-bag and listened to the thunderclaps increase in volume and frequency, I anxiously hoped they would make it quickly off the water onto a campsite. Twilight had turned to night, and the storm was closing in.

Distant white flickers began to be visible. Within fifteen minutes these had become dazzling lightning flashes, almost immediately followed by what sounded like bomb blasts. The wind also came up suddenly, thrashing branches of the evergreens around frantically. You don't argue with nature. I tidied up on the double, locked the food barrel, and dove into my tent at 9:00, just as the first big splattering raindrops fell.

In minutes the storm was raging directly overhead. Thunderclaps and blinding flashbulbs as bright as day exploded simultaneously. My little yellow tent held true, but its top flapped several times, as if alive. Like some large creature, breathing in, filling itself to almost burst, it would then exhale until its sides became concave. I pulled my things away from the edges as the splendour and power of nature took over. Although I believed I was safe huddled in my shelter, I was aware of my fragility. It almost felt as if I was back in the river again, surrounded by rushing water. Several times when the lightning flashes and thunder burst, I simultaneously felt the ground quake underneath me. A deluge of hard rain pelted for half an hour, as the climax of the storm peaked. At last the frenzy subsided. The downpour suddenly eased off, then stopped. The sound-and-light show rolled off somewhere into the distance, and everything became quiet, dripping, humid. I closed my eyes and tried to sleep.

My plan before the storm hit, had been to lie in the tent and enjoy the sound of the rapids that night, as I had done at that same site last year, and many places before. Other than the rough night of my accident at Rollway, I've always loved that lullaby. Now I was back on the river, with new hope, a new boat, rebuilt confidence, and maybe even a bit of increased wisdom, ready to enjoy the sound again. But, as it turned out, there would be no listening to the song of the rapids that first night back on the Petawawa. In total, a line of three big storms closely followed one another, and the many diverse sounds of rain dominated most of the night. When I'm camping, it's okay with me if it rains after dark. All that new water would bump up the river's flow a bit. But I hoped those other campers were alright.

Another custom I occasionally follow is to listen to the river. At those times, I don't just listen to the wonderful sounds made by the water, but also try to imagine if there might be a voice or voices actually whispering, or somehow communicating with me, in a way that I can understand. I try to hear whatever message the water might give me. This can be done on or beside, either flat or moving water. My rational brain understands that this type of activity is a form of personal introspection or meditation. But who knows, there might also be some kind of mystical aspect. It's surprising what can be heard, if you listen.

During that night of storms, as with the white noise of the rapids, any potential whisperings were drowned out. Going to sleep, I told myself to remember in the morning, while paddling the first flat stretch coming up, to take some time to listen.

End of the Portage

12

I allowed myself to sleep in as long as the trees were dripping, and so didn't crawl out of the tent until 8:30. The air was warm and still. The luminous atmosphere seemed to consist of a single, low, white cloud that started just above my head. Clear air near the ground transformed upwards into fog, and the treetops disappeared into a shining, bright white light. As I took my first steps, I felt soft mud and wet spruce needles squish under my paddling shoes. Everything was sopping. Jewel drops of rainwater hung everywhere, waiting to fall with the first breeze. After so many dry, hot days, everything had been given a long, thirst-quenching drink. It seemed as if it might rain more any second, or who knows, it might not rain at all. Either way, this was going to be a special day.

Despite my usual ease at making fires, it took a full twenty minutes to get one going. My favourite trick, of starting with a small bundle of dry twigs collected from thin low dead branches of evergreens, was a damp dud. To find anything truly dry, I had to use my PFD knife and carve shavings off a stick. Fortunately, the inner chips were enough to get a small flame going. More whittled wood and the driest dead twigs I could find, eventually produced a reluctant smoky fire, with just enough heat to boil water for breakfast and coffee. Woodsmoke on a warm, damp morning seems to have a particularly sweet fragrance. With the air so still, and the low white cloud, the smoke floated only a short distance above my little camp, as if in an old illustration of some fairy tale scene.

As I packed up, I moved slowly, thoughtfully, remembering. This was going to be my "return to the scene" day. I aimed to reach the site of my wreck by mid-afternoon, then camp at the top of the Rollway portage, using the same site that had served as my emergency refuge. The plan was to get up the next morning, portage my gear and also my canoe down the trail, and continue my journey. But with the low cloud, and the weather looking unsettled, I knew my timing needed to be flexible.

After dousing what was left of the embers with a bailer full of water, and carrying everything to the end of the short Little Thompson trail, I paddled away at 11:00. A few minutes after starting, feeling calm and pensive, I rested my paddle across the gunwales, sat back on the seat with my knees up, and let the boat drift. The gentle current in that long smooth section of the river carried me slowly along. After a couple of minutes I lay right back on the airbag, completely relaxed. Except for an occasional dip-and-drag to steer, it was a free ride. I can't remember if I closed my eyes for a while, but I did let myself go into a very pleasant daydream for at least twenty minutes. It was the kind of dream that visits my thoughts now and then, of being like a lotus floating on the water, gently cradled on a calm, pristine summer river, feeling at one with nature. On this day, the dream was real.

As the canoe drifted, I listened to the river. That morning it seemed to somehow quietly convey a simple message: "Go carefully, and with respect, remembering what has gone before, and what will come after, and you'll be fine." Good advice.

Eventually I came back to focusing on reaching my destination, sat back up, and started to paddle. I continued four or five kilometres to the first swift in a peaceful mood. I thought of some things coming up, and some things gone by. But mainly I soaked in the present. As I travelled, the low white ceiling of morning cloud gradually lifted, and the hot, hazy summer sun began to burn through.

Besides being a different river every day, the Petawawa also has a unique character in each section. That five-kilometre smooth stretch is one that I always think of as having mainly green borders, and a few small islands. The pleasant help given by the current makes it flow as if it's a slow-speed flume ride, so paddling can remain easy and gentle. The boat floated gracefully past tall pines and cedars that grow right to the river's edge. Iconic tree shapes and several shades of deep green were complemented here and there by the lighter, brighter greens of low ferns and other plants that often formed a narrow rim along the water. This is classic Canadian Shield country. The many characteristic shore boulders again made me wish I could capture the scene in a painting, but a memory imprint had to suffice.

As I cruised past each campsite, I looked for the eight paddlers who had passed through my camp before the storm, but there was no sign. They must have stayed at one of the sites, gotten up early, and left. I never saw them again, so I guess they did alright.

The first short moving water of the day was a shallow swift, an easy gentle run. Lasting only a couple of minutes, and needing no special navigating skills, it was still great to be moving quickly through rushing water again. In a couple more kilometres, my paddling confidence was given a further boost as I easily navigated the longer, slightly more challenging run, called Grillade Rapids. Smiling, I told myself, "I can do this – carefully, and with respect."

I then settled back and enjoyed the next short paddle to the top of the long, and potentially quite dangerous Crooked Chute Rapids. No-one should ever paddle the Petawawa without a good map or two, but even with a map, the Crooked Chute area is a place where every traveler must use extreme caution. It's compulsory to pull over, get out, scout carefully, and think with a clear head.

Over a kilometre and a half long, the Crooked Chute Rapids are beautiful, but they get harder and more dangerous as a boat zigzags along. It looks easy at first, but as the water descends along its bending staircase, the difficulty level goes steadily up, from an initial Class 1, up to Class 2, and then reaches a deadly spot where it jumps right off the scale to "Don't Run!"

The very real danger facing someone who chooses to run the first part, is that they might easily miss the last chance to take-out before the actual roaring chute. This small, tricky-to-hit last take-out is on river-right, and there's a quick must-do maneuver required to make it. If a paddler misses it, they will be immediately and inescapably swept around a thundering, deep, high-speed, 120º hairpin turn. The water will slam-dunk them against a sheer rock wall and capsize them. But it won't end there. They will then be pummeled down half a kilometre of twisting aerated whitewater and large boulders. Any of these multiple hazards will injure them, almost certainly wreck their boat, and possibly kill them.

In good conditions, experienced paddlers are often able to slowly and carefully paddle down to that last chance take-out spot, and safely get off the water. Some people portage around the chute section then put back in and run the bottom part of the rapids. But for most people, it is definitely safest to portage the entire kilometre-and-a-half, even though it's a long carry. I had scouted the full length of the long Crooked Chute Rapids before on other trips, including the previous year, and remembered it well, but still got out at the first portage sign and scouted it again.

On this déjà vu day, as with the day of my wreck the previous August, two thirds of the way along the portage trail there was a small official-looking red octagonal "ARRET - STOP" sign on a tree beside the water at that last chance take-out. Pieces of wrecked boats had also been left there this year, as cautions. Still, that little sign could easily be missed by a busy or frantic paddler. I also wouldn't count on any sign at all necessarily still being there in other years, so prior scouting is always essential. Heaven help the person who finds themselves in the middle of the river, or on the left side, or for any reason unable to pull their boat out on the right as they approach the hairpin chute. My advice to paddlers is: Don't even think about running it! Pull out and take the portage. Live to sit on the beautiful big rocks beside the chute, and gaze at this wonderful "power place."

The huge rocks right beside the tight turn are a fabulous spot to watch the river fly by. I usually like to have an extended lunch break there, but had foolishly rushed past it the previous year, trying to get to the Big Cliffs campsite. That rushing hadn't paid off. Not stopping to rest was a mistake I wouldn't repeat.

When I refer to the hairpin turn of Crooked Chute as a power place, I'm not talking about hydro. Thank goodness this part of the river and its watershed has been protected by its Algonquin Provincial Park status for over a hundred years. Electricity-seekers would surely have dammed it long ago right there at Crooked Chute. Even today, probably some would jump at a chance to do this if it weren't protected. Like so many rapids and falls all over the world, this beautiful inspiring place would have been drowned. The long rapids would be just a memory, and the old riverbed lost, buried somewhere under deep flat water, at the bottom of a reservoir lake. Either that, or all the rocks of the former historic rapids might be left exposed and dry, below some dam. But, thankfully, due to conservation efforts both past and present, the Petawawa still runs freely. Yes, I use electricity, but I'm thankful that not all rivers are dammed.

During my scout of Crooked Chute, I confirmed what I had expected. The current water level was good: not too high or too low. I had run the first part safely several times, including the previous year: paddling carefully around the first long bend, then rock dodging along the right, while keeping my speed slow with lots of back-paddling and a couple of back-ferries. This ensured that I could safely pull my boat out quickly at that last STOP point. On this déjà vu day, I counted only a few risk lemons, and knew I had the knowledge and skills to go. Still, I thought a long time about perhaps portaging my gear all the way, but in the end, decided that, with the good water level, things should be okay.

The *Waterwalker* music started in my head. I kept the volume low as I slowly and carefully lined up the canoe and paddled through the first beautiful sections of whitewater. My new Mad River navigated the twists and turns just as smoothly and easily as my old one, without incident. I carefully guided the canoe down to that last river-right take-out, abruptly stopped, hopped out, and pulled her up onto shore. I'm no rodeo star, but I couldn't have felt more pleased. Standing there alone in the wild, beside my canoe, I felt a rush of exhilaration stronger than I had felt in a year. It wasn't bravado, just deep inner satisfaction.

The long Crooked Chute portage trail, which begins about a kilometre upriver, at the first yellow "Mister Canoehead" sign, passes through the STOP sign area, then veers off to the right for its last leg down to the very end of the rapids. This remaining section is roughly half a kilometre, or one third of the trail's entire length. I first carried my canoe down to the end of the portage and left it there, ready and waiting, sitting on the shore. Besides enjoying the songbirds and forest greenery on my hike back up, I looked forward to taking a break before the second walk, when I would carry all my gear down. This time I wouldn't pass up the opportunity to take in the thrilling scene at the chute.

When I arrived back at my gear, I had the good fortune of running into two women paddlers just as they emerged from the top section of the trail. One was carrying their canoe, and the other their packs. They put everything down near the stop sign, and we said hello and gave brief introductions. They were in the process of portaging the entire Crooked Chute rapid, all the way from the first take-out. Currently on day eight of their twelve-day Algonquin Park trip, I was surprised to hear them say they weren't running any of the rapids along the way, because they felt they didn't have sufficient whitewater paddling skills.

They thought they had caught a couple of glimpses of me far ahead of them earlier in the day, starting somewhere below Little Thompson, but hadn't been sure if the few small flashes of red were indeed a boat. I thought to myself that perhaps it was just after I had been floating like a lotus on the water. We decided they must have approached the take-out at the start of the Little Thompson portage perhaps half an hour to an hour after I checked out of the site, and had roughly kept pace with me all the way along. We exchanged cameras and took each other's photographs standing by the STOP sign. Leaving the heavy work for later, we grabbed our lunches and walked down the side trail to the chute together, to share our break on the huge rocks.

Small rapids make a hissing noise. Big ones make a rumble. The hairpin turn of Crooked Chute makes a loud roar. The thundering water seems more alive than ever. When sitting perched on the bedrock beside the spectacle, the turmoil has a vitality that rubs off. The force of the water is not only heard, but also felt, vibrating on your chest, and in the trembling of the large outcrop of Canadian Shield rock on which you sit. There's extra oxygen in the air, and the spray feels like the very breath of the river. It moistens your face and hands, and softens the air in your lungs. Sitting there always brings me complex feelings that are difficult to understand or label, but at the minimum, there is a combination of awe, inspiration, grace, timelessness, and gratitude. It awakens something in my soul.

People who've been fortunate enough to visit this spot, will probably understand what I mean when I label it a power place. You can feel it. There is a sense that one is present at a touchstone, an area that has been considered special for a very long time. The place has spirit.

As the funnelling river roared past just below our feet, the three of us sat and chatted like old friends about our personal journeys. It was such a pleasant time. I told them of my difficulties last August, and my plan for the present trip. That very afternoon I would be back at the scene. They told me about their own fabulous summer-long camping plans which, after the Algonquin Park part, included a trip to Wabakimi Provincial Park. On their recommendation, I added this to my list of places to visit, and in turn recommended they visit Pukaskwa National Park on their way past. We shared our treats. Their dried turkey was delicious. When I mentioned my plan to go carefully and with respect, one of them noted, quite correctly, that this is always a good idea, whenever doing anything in nature.

It's been my experience that river trippers are usually wonderful people. I enjoy sometimes travelling solo but I'm happy to occasionally run into other travellers like these two, and make quick friends. During our brief shared time by the chute we connected immediately. Yet if we had passed on a city street I'm sure we would never have talked, let alone sat and shared our lunches, plans, and a few dreams. Happily, on the river, there's no problem. It just feels natural. There's nothing to fear, no worries. We're all just paddlers, sharing a little of ourselves.

After lunch, the three of us finished the portage, then loaded our canoes and paddled side-by-side for the two kilometres from the bottom of Crooked Chute to the top of Rollway. Just after we launched, I cut off a piece of the sweetgrass braid and gave it to them to keep. We burned a little of my remaining piece, letting the smoke drift over us, as I told them the teachings I had learned.

Memory tapes from last year played vividly as we drifted past the ranger cabin. My gaze focussed on the spot where I had sat with others around the fire, the night before my long hike out. I thought of the water-walking ATV driver from the far shore, and the "bicycle family." As our two canoes passed together through the little swift, I remembered the up-river journey with my rescuers, and their kindness and generosity.

Accompanied by those two men when I left to go upriver last year, and by these two women as I returned on this beautiful summer day, I felt blessed, almost escorted. Because of our serendipitous meeting, and the relaxed time the two women and I had spent together at the chute, I didn't have to paddle in alone, as I returned to Rollway.

We pulled our boats out at the yellow Mister Canoehead portage sign, the one where I had left my paper warning about the hazard in the river. I told my friends I would come to the bottom of the path in about twenty minutes and hopefully see them off if they were still there. They loaded themselves up, carrying everything in one trip again, and left. I hauled my gear and canoe over to the little trailhead campsite. It looked much the same. With mixed emotions, I then walked down along that familiar portage trail, toward the scene of my wreck.

Looking from the high bank on this new day almost a year later, the considerably deeper river flowed right over the top of what had been the flat, dry, black riverbed. Of course, there was no pinned red boat, no boat at all, no piece of ABS plastic or splinter of wood, no shred of rope, no remnant whatsoever. Everything was gone. Only the river remained; the river and my memories.

Even the two large rocks that had caused me such trouble were gone, invisible, buried deep under the present medium-high water. I walked a little further and looked down, from the place by the cross. The presence of those two hidden rocks was barely revealed by a couple of tell-tale curves on the surface. An unloaded canoe would easily float right over them.

Another big circle was complete. I was back, but in many ways had already moved on. So, of course, had the river. My old Mad River was long gone, as I had always known it would be. But I was still standing, and had, as promised, returned with my new boat, to finish my journey.

After watching for several minutes, as the water poured over the long ledge, I couldn't help turning around and staring for a while at the little cross. I don't really know where all my blessings and good fortunes have come from. They probably arrive from many different and complicated sources. But I do know I've been very fortunate to receive them. Often, I take my good fortune too much for granted. I'm never really sure who or what to thank, but when I look back over my life, I feel deep gratitude. That, I think, is the important thing: to feel thankful inside. How a person chooses to direct that feeling is up to them. Standing by that Rollway shore once more, I was thankful to have been able to leave, to get home safely, to have been able to come back with a new boat, and to have the chance to continue on.

Two weeks after my accident, I had already known there would be nothing left of my broken canoe. The heavy remnant winds and rains of mighty Hurricane Katrina were still quite strong when it doused Ontario during that first week of September, after causing wide-spread catastrophes in the US. That would have raised the water level of the Petawawa considerably, and floated the wreck off the rock.

My own difficulties last August paled to insignificance as I stood looking at the cross, remembering stories of the horror and tragedy that hundreds of thousands had faced when Katrina and the hurricane-swollen ocean breeched the New Orleans levees on August 29, 2005, flooding the city, and homes all along the Gulf of Mexico coast. Eighteen hundred people dead from one storm. Their circles broken.

Later last autumn, there had been even more strong storms and torrential rains throughout Ontario. They too would have repeatedly flooded the Petawawa, as the worst hurricane season in history played out. Rains, winds, winter jams of ice, and spring floodwaters would have easily done to the remains of my old canoe what I could not.

And that wouldn't have been the end. There would likely have been many more scrapes and crashes. Repeated further pinning must have marked her trail as, over days, weeks and months, she lumbered and smashed along the last 300 metres of rock-studded Rollway, and perhaps further downriver. Stripped of her airbags and wood, she would probably have eventually sunk, and finally been wedged somewhere deep, buried in the water. Remnants would still be there, somewhere in the dark. The best I could hope for was that maybe some-one might have hauled the hull, or pieces of it, into the bush somewhere along the river. But, there was nothing. No trace.

I shook away dark thoughts, and confidently told myself, "I will go on from here, and finish this time. I'll bring my new boat back whole and tell Jill how everything was wonderful." I reminded myself of the little flock of small birds that had flown over me, and helped fill me with hope when I was so afraid, standing in the middle of the river last summer. Some birds like that were probably still around, somewhere nearby.

At the end of the trail, I said goodbye to the two Crooked Chute women. They thanked me again for the sweetgrass, and pushed off, waving behind them on the fly. They were on their way, continuing their journey, and I was alone again, continuing mine.

I'm quite aware that it's often hard for me to let go of things I feel strongly about. Walking back up to the little campsite, I again obsessively scouted every bit of the rivershore back to the wreck site, just in case. It was no surprise that there was nothing. Not even a single chip of red plastic. Everything was gone, long gone down the river. Still, I was happy to be back, able to see the place again with my own eyes. Among other feelings, I was experiencing closure.

I set my little tent up on the same spot as last year, but this time feeling comfortable, fortunate and satisfied. It was sunny and 5:00, not dark, rainy and 9:00. I wasn't trembling. There was no emergency. Only memories and plans, and a beautiful summer afternoon. I took the evening slow and easy, and went into the tent early.

After writing in my journal, I lay quietly, looking over one of my replacement maps. Then, on my camera, I scanned through the photographs taken by Jill and I during our wonderful five days on Lake Travers. Such good times.

As I nodded off, I watched about twenty small, pale white butterflies flutter up, one at a time, under the top of my tent fly. I could see them walking around, between the mesh of the inner tent and the outer nylon fly. After casually observing them gathering for a while, I realized these little butterflies, or moths, were collecting in this cozy dry spot in order to have shelter from any possible rain in the night. Another evening thunderstorm did rumble past later on somewhere nearby, but it didn't rain on me. I rested peacefully, enjoying the song of the rapids once more.

I really liked watching those little butterflies. My mom had passed away at the beginning of the summer, less than a month before I retired. I had thought about her a lot during some of the quiet times on Travers, and during these first two solo days back on the river. Her deep love of nature had nurtured me throughout my life, and continues to enrich me and my children. She also generously shared her love of nature with hundreds of young people that she influenced over the years as a leader of youth groups and at summer camps.

A year or so before she died, I offered to do a painting for her. I asked her to tell me seven things she would like to see in the picture, so I could create what I call a "Seven Wishes painting." She chose to see Jill and I, in our two red boats, on a lake in Algonquin Park, with pines, a loon, and the surrounding shorelines and forested hills. I painted the two of us paddling on Lake Travers. My Mom expressed sadness at not being able to canoe any more, but said that whenever she looked at the painting, it made her feel good. I hung her Seven Wishes painting on the wall at the foot of her bed, in her room in the nursing home, so she could look at it anytime. This of course made me happy. Sadly, it came back to me too soon.

My mother loved butterflies and angels, and they have always been strongly connected with her in my mind. She had large collections of butterfly and angel trinkets. The concept of metamorphosis meant a great deal to her. The small pale white visitors that gathered above me in my tent reminded me of that, and made me think of her, and everything she had done for me. As I went to sleep at the end of my return-to-the-scene day. I didn't feel afraid, or alone. Maybe she was somehow nearby, as she probably always is. Maybe there is more to metamorphosis than we think. Certainly, that flock of small butterflies was right there, resting like a cluster of little angels above me.

Despite these pleasant thoughts, I was surprised to still be woken in the middle of the night by visceral replays of last year's ordeal. Twice I found myself back in the middle of it all: taking an ultra-slow-motion step out of the boat down into the current, struggling to keep standing in rushing water to my neck, permanently releasing my grip and abandoning ship, pulling on ropes that wouldn't budge, cutting the lines, staggering under my load up that long trail, trying to get home. These, and things I can't bring myself to write, whirled through me. But thankfully, it only happened twice. And this year, each time I woke, they vanished. Because there I was, truly safe and sound, with increased caution and my new boat.

End of the Portage

13

Looking out the door of my tent in the morning, everything looked perfect. Other than a little dew, the campsite was dry. I pulled on my old white "Canada Rocks" T-shirt, the one with five red Inuksuk in a vertical yellow column that always reminds me of my family. I'd been wearing it when the wreck happened, and would wear it again on this day, as I paddled on. My objective was to finally make it to the big Natch Cliffs campsite that afternoon, and camp there.

The cool night air in my tent had been steadily warmed by the early sun, and it was beginning to get a little hot in there as I crawled out. Little birds chirped away. The sky was cerulean blue. I felt fantastic.

During breakfast, I noticed that, as expected, the small piece of sweetgrass I had left on the fire circle rock last August was no longer there. Perhaps it had become part of someone else's story. I cupped my hands around my third cup of coffee, wandered up to the head of the portage, and stood there awhile, looking upriver. This was where last year's homeward journey had started. A lot had happened since then. Looking at my watch I saw that it was almost 10:00 a.m. I smiled when I noticed the date: July the eleventh: "7-11" - surely a lucky day!

Back at the campsite, I emptied the tent and began taking it down. I had forgotten all about the pale white butterflies. Once all the pegs had been removed from the fly, I gave it a quick lift and flick up in the air, like a bedsheet. Suddenly out burst a flurry of at least twenty little butterflies. They flew about, circling around my head briefly, then fluttering upwards. I was completely bedazzled. My last view of them was high above me, as each one twinkled in the sun, then seemed to disappear. In seconds, all of them were gone. It was one of the neatest things I've ever seen in nature. I felt like a magician, who had ceremoniously waved his cape and made eye-popping magic. I couldn't help taking this as another good sign, and thought again of my mom, angels, and metamorphosis.

By 11:00 I was all packed and had no-traced the site. I portaged the canoe and gear two thirds of the way down the trail, to the small put-in just below the cross. With the present good water level, I knew it would be safe to hop in there, and ride the last third of Rollway.

As I was about to get in, two couples came walking down the portage trail. We chatted a few minutes and they said they were continuing down past my put-in spot, portaging all their gear to the very end of the trail. The two men were scouting the rapids as they went, preparing to go back and do two tandem runs down the full length of Rollway in their empty canoes. Empty canoes, I thought: good plan!

The higher water level this summer meant fewer exposed rocks, but Rollway is always challenging. Although they looked experienced, as a courtesy I offered to act as a safety person for them, and stand on the shore beside my ready canoe, holding my rescue throwbag prepared to toss, just in case. They were happy to take the offer, so I delayed my journey half an hour.

The women and I had a great view as the men executed an excellent safe run in their first canoe. My throwbag stayed dry, and instead of doing any rescuing, I took several photos. The boat floated easily through the high-volume V in the ledge, and directly over the two, now-submerged rocks, that had caused me difficulty. After sailing past me, I watched as they skillfully rock-dodged the final 300 metres to the end of the rapids, then pulled their canoe out on river-right, in the calmer deep section that I had swum across to retrieve my pack and tent. They secured the boat beside their waiting gear, and started hiking back up the trail to do the second run in their other canoe. I was envious, but again reminded myself that I was intentionally playing it extra safe this time. On their way by me, we all agreed that with this water level, and their first canoe now waiting at the end, it was safe for me to leave and continue my trip. After getting an email address to send pictures, I said goodbye.

My new boat was waiting. So was the river. I stepped in, and with a rush of adrenalin and joy, pushed off. Instantly the strong current swept me along. With a few quick manoeuvres, the final third of Rollway flew by without a single splash coming in.

As I floated beyond the rapids, through the first flatwater section, I caught myself still obsessively scanning both shores for any bit of red, until finally acceptance settled inside. Those difficult times were behind me now.

A kilometre later I portaged my gear, and easily ran both sets of the beautiful Natch Rapids in my empty canoe. Loading the boat up again, a little further along I quietly paddled through the last short rapid. This easy set is located just before the river widens, and becomes like a small lake for roughly a kilometre. There, it slows down and flows past the Natch

Cliffs camping area on river-left. It was early afternoon. The deeper, calmer, wider water assured me I had arrived at one of the most spectacular areas on the Petawawa. Placing my paddle across the gunwales to let the boat drift, I sat back on the seat, savouring the moment. In the distance a couple of ravens called.

The lake-like area is surrounded by outstanding natural beauty. I think it must be memorable to anyone who sees it. I'm sure people have considered it special for thousands of years. As I drifted, I watched with anticipation, knowing that quite soon the towering 100-metre grey, white, black and orange cliffs, plummeting to the river's edge on both sides of the water, would loom into view. Suddenly, there they were.

As a bonus, there was no-one to be seen or heard anywhere. Both of the excellent campsites by the water were wide open. If the two women who had waved goodbye to me at the bottom of Rollway had camped there the previous night, they had already left.

The first site has lovely, old, leaning cedar trees, and some very large boulders that look as if they were randomly tossed there by giants. I refer to it as the "Cedars" campsite. Although the smaller of the two sites, there is still plenty of room to set up three or four tents among the scattered large rocks. There are also lovely views along the water to the giant cliffs.

The second, and much larger site, is about 150 metres further along on the same river-left shore. It's quite a bit closer to the cliffs, so I call it the "big Natch Cliffs" campsite, or simply the "Big Cliffs" site. It's my favourite place to sleep on the whole river. I know how most campers have their own preferred camping spot. Mine is right there, surrounded by several huge white pines and cedars, looking out on the clean, deep river, and those magnificent cliffs. I also appreciate the fact that a person has to work hard to get there. It's definitely paddle-in camping. There are wonderful stretches of rapids a paddler must travel through or around before arriving, and further long stretches to ride, coming up downriver. To me, this area is the heart, the essence of the Petawawa, where the wildness feels strongest.

Not surprisingly, it's a popular stop-over area, so it was a treat to have my pick of both sites. I had no trouble choosing. Delighted, I pulled my new Mad River in at the take-out spot by the Big Cliffs site, directly below a huge white pine that has the orange Algonquin Park campsite sign posted. After securing the boat, and taking a brief walk around to check out the site and pick up a few small left-over bits of garbage, I unloaded everything, and set up my tent.

Some of those white pines are so old and large, they were probably there as young trees back in the logging days. Somehow they had been spared by the cutting crews who used this place as their camp for awhile. For millennia before that, I'm sure First Nations peoples also stayed at, or near, this location by the foot of the huge cliffs. In those times, all the pine and cedar would have been virgin trees. I can only imagine what the forest must have looked like.

Sleeping or resting on the scented mat of soft pine needles that covers the ground at this site always comes easily to me. I angled one door of my tent so I could lie and look at the fabulous view of giant pines with the enormous backdrop of the cliffs.

The earth around the main clearing there, and in parts of the large tenting area, has a curious acoustic quality that adds to the uniqueness of this special campsite. If you stomp on the ground, it sounds almost hollow, and makes a booming sound which resonates, like the beating of a very large drum. I don't know the cause.

If there are a lot of people travelling on the river, it's always proper protocol to share a big site like this. I expected I would probably have the good fortune of welcoming other paddlers to join me later in the afternoon. But when I had finished setting up, it was still fairly early, only just after 2:00, and I was the only person who had checked in. I enjoyed a pleasant time of solitude, sitting on the large bedrock outcropping located beside the water, flanked by two of the largest pines. I gazed up at the cliffs and across the calm water, revelling in my good fortune, my spirit savouring fulfilment.

In the afternoon stillness, somewhere high on the cliffs, two ravens called back and forth intermittently. Perhaps they were the same two that had welcomed me to the area. The sheer rock walls gave their throaty voices an additional fullness and reverberation. A few small birds chipped and flitted down low in some riverside bushes, reminding me of Lake Travers. Now and then, a skinny little blue dragonfly cruised by, its wings making the sound of rattling cellophane.

After sitting less than ten minutes, I heard a flutter of wings close behind me. A whiskey jack, also called a grey jay, had landed. It must have spotted me from somewhere near the campsite. Accustomed to generous or careless visitors, it was probably hoping for a morsel, but this time had to fly away disappointed.

The heat of the perfect day, and the quiet calm of the wide section of almost calm water called to me to come for a swim, and I couldn't refuse. After doing some lazy breast strokes out to the middle, I rolled over to float on my back, and gaze upwards. A few small white wisps of clouds drifted very slowly in the blue sky, high above the clifftops. I closed my eyes for a minute, floating, at peace. When I opened them again, those magnificent cliffs, the gorgeous big pines, and my canoe resting by the campsite were all still there. It wasn't a dream.

Stepping out, I stood and drip-dried in the sunlight a few minutes, then finished the job using my customary camp towel, which is to say, a T-shirt, in this case my "Canada Rocks" one. I smiled again. Canada rocks indeed. Since the day was quite warm, the pat-down only made the shirt feel a little damp, so I just put it back on. After finishing getting dressed, I realized I hadn't eaten any lunch, so went over and started rummaging around in the food barrel looking for something easy.

While doing this, I heard a little bump. It was a barely audible thud. But in the still air, it was that soft, distant sound that lets a camper know they have company. I started walking toward the other campsite to see who had arrived, fully expecting it would be the four people I met on Rollway in the morning, but I was wrong. When almost there, I met a solo paddler who had left his canoe pulled up at the Cedars. He was walking toward me, on his way to check out the situation at the big site.

We greeted each other cheerfully, and I invited him to share the large campsite with me. He politely declined, preferring to be on his own. I understood the solo preference. We both remarked how unusual it was for two lone paddlers to meet like this.

His name was Nelson, and he was from Hamilton. I told him my name, and that I was from Ottawa. This is pretty much the extent of introductions needed when solo paddlers meet on a river. He was friendly and seemed close to my age. After going back to his canoe, he brought back some food, and I got some of mine from the barrel. The two of us shared, as we sat and chatted around the big fire circle of that beautiful campsite, eating our late lunches. I told him the main points of my trip the previous year, and how at the time that I wiped out, I had been wearing this same T- shirt, and had been trying to get to this campsite.

As travellers often do, we then continued with other trip stories, trading memorable paddling experiences. Somehow it came out that about fifteen years ago, Nelson had paddled the fabulous Mountain River in the Northwest Territories with a group.

On his Mountain River trip, Nelson, and the paddlers he was with, had heard news of another group, who had gone down the same wild river only a week or two ahead of them, riding exceptionally high floodwaters from several days of heavy rain in the mountains. That group had run into serious trouble. Early in their trip, one of their rental canoes wiped out and wrapped like a banana peel around a large rock in pounding, deep, frigid current. He and his friends also heard that by the next day, the other group's canoe had completely disappeared, drowned under the rising waters of a flash flood, the type common in steep mountain valleys after heavy rain. It took a few days of difficult group work but, as the water level went down, they constructed a small partial dam out of many hundreds of rocks rolled down the mountainside, and managed to temporarily deflect part of the Mountain River's strong current. They had then been able to recover their bent and flattened plastic boat, and amazingly, were also able to repair it quickly, allowing all of them to keep paddling, and successfully complete their trip.

I listened in stunned silence. I could hardly believe it! This man, now travelling solo along the Petawawa like myself, and meeting me by chance here at the Big Cliffs campsite, was describing my own memorable canoe journey with a group of friends on the Mountain River in 1991. The wreck he had heard about, was my own canoe, my serious wipe out and fortunate recovery with my paddling partner Roger. It was actually on a tributary leading to the Mountain River, at a place our group came to call Eagle Rock. After listening in astonishment while he related my own story back to me, I confessed that the boat he had heard about, all those years ago, had been mine.

After each of us had done further confirmation of facts, mutual amazement sank in. We must have gone down the Mountain River, at the most, two weeks apart, fifteen summers ago! Small world indeed! Now here we were, many years and trips later, sitting together around the fire circle at this very special campsite on the Petawawa. And Nelson had been canoeing a short distance behind me once again.

I was humbled and embarrassed to have told him that last summer I had wrapped a second canoe. We could hardly believe the coincidences. After laughing and shaking our heads several times, we settled into telling some of our less dramatic trip stories. I tried to convince him that I really don't go around wrecking canoes all the time. Two in fifteen years of extensive paddling wasn't that bad was it? Well, yes, actually it was. It was something I wasn't proud of, and planned to avoid ever doing again.

I told him that when my Mountain River rental canoe was recovered and repaired enough to enable us to finish our trip, we had dubbed her "The Mary Ellen Carter the Second," after the wonderful Stan Rogers song.[4] We had indeed made that Mountain River boat "rise again." But sadly, my fourteen-year-old Mad River, wrecked upriver the previous August, would not be recovered.

---

4 "*The Mary Ellen Carter*" – Stan Rogers (SOCAN) c p Fogarty's Cove Music 1979

Nelson told me he had paddled all the way from Lake Travers that day. As he came out of the big lake in the morning, he chatted with a young couple who were on their honeymoon. They were paddling a brand new red Starburst canoe, which they had been given as a fabulous wedding gift. He thought they might arrive at this Big Cliffs area later, and be looking for a place to camp. I told him that, like himself, they were quite welcome to share the big site. There was plenty of room. He again thanked me, but said he preferred to set up on his own, at the Cedars campsite.

We agreed to talk more, and he left to set up his tent. I planned to sort my barrel a bit, then lie down for a little rest. But just before I got into my tent, I saw Nelson walk back along the path with his large canoe pack. When he had returned to the Cedars, he found out that a family with two 'mango'-coloured canoes had paddled in. Since they were the bigger group, he graciously let them have the site. I wasn't surprised when still, instead of camping near me, he chose to pitch his little tent roughly half way between my site and the one with the family.

The tiny level clearing he chose was barely big enough to fit the footprint of his tent. It was only a couple of metres from the river's edge, right beside a very old, semi-floating jam of tree trunks, branches, beaver muck and live grassy plants that juts straight out four or five metres into the water. It looks a little like a very rough natural dock or raft. Besides the evidence of live grasses growing on parts of it, I knew this collection of natural river debris was old, because I had seen it, or similar configurations, in the same location on previous trips, although I'd never seen anyone camp beside it. The little clearing isn't an official third tent site, but rather more like an extension, or fringe of the large campsite. Nelson said he was fine with sleeping there one night, and would be leaving in the morning. He was very environmentally conscious, and said that to ensure he didn't damage the fragile riverside environment near the tent, he would use the fire area of my big site for all his cooking, eating, and general camp activities.

I went over to my tent again to have a lie-down, but it was pretty hot inside. After about ten minutes, I decided to get up and visit one of my favourite local touchstone spots, another power place. Located only about 50 metres from the main campsite clearing, it can be easily found in a couple of minutes, on the brim of a small rocky hillock of cedar and pine that rises five or six metres. Looking over the crest, a low cliff face drops to the water below, and there at the top, cut into the sheer solid rock by nature alone, is a perfect small sitting place I call the "Stone Throne." I try to visit it every time I pass by.

To me, and I'm sure many others, it looks like a large square seat with high arms. It must have been somehow cut there by natural forces thousands of years ago, yet gives the impression of always being ready and waiting for an occupant. Stepping carefully over the brink, one can sit comfortably in this natural chair, and feel privileged for a while, like a king or queen, or more appropriately, a chief.

Probably countless individuals have sat or stood in the Stone Throne, since time immemorial. There are splendid views of the tall cliffs opposite, the lake-like area, and the narrowing path of the departing river. At times when there is no wind, the river reflects beautiful mirror images of the cliffs. When foggy, hints of giant rock faces sometimes loom out of the mist.

I sat down and quietly remembered earlier trips. For solid stone, it is surprisingly comfortable and conducive to letting the mind drift. I'm sure many other occupants have found themselves in a meditative mood there, pondering their lives, sorting through issues, making plans, recalling memories, having dreams, or perhaps writing. I thought of First Nations individuals and groups passing through, or maybe living in the area, for many millennia before the coming of Europeans. During more recent history, there were groups of loggers, then many thousands of park visitors, both famous and unknown. Tom Thomson did paintings of these huge Petawawa cliffs a few times in 1916. Although I can't prove it, it's my belief that at least one of his paintings was done while he was in the Stone Throne. No doubt hundreds of other artists have painted there, sketched, or taken outstanding photographs. Remembering this, I pulled my little digital camera out of my pocket and took a few pictures.

But the Stone Throne is only part, one half of an outstanding pair of lookouts. There is another power place very close by, a high viewpoint I call "Lookout Rock." It sits on the top of almost the tallest section of the big cliffs. This second natural wonder gives an eagle-eye perspective of the whole valley area, including splendid views up and down the river, and a direct line of sight to the Stone Throne. It's as if nature lined up these two lookouts, so that when there are people present in both, they can see each other.

Because it's perched so high, Lookout Rock can be observed, not only from the Stone Throne, but from practically anywhere on the water or in the campsites area. It is a large chunk of rock with an almost level top, located 100 metres above the river, at the crest of the cliff. To an observer below, it can appear as if this huge rock is precariously held in place solely by a large "pebble" wedged underneath. This pebble is actually a very big rock, but it is many times smaller than the massive slab it seems to support. The impression is that this pivotal boulder is barely able to prevent Lookout Rock from plummeting straight down and crashing into the river. But this impression is false. Science tells us that besides the entire area being under a saltwater sea half a billion years ago, both the large slab and its small supporting partner have been perched there on the clifftop together for thousands of years.[5]

When I stare up at Lookout Rock from far below, or gaze down from it while standing like a sentinel on its top, I'm humbled by time and space. I feel awe and wonder, similar to times when I gaze at stars from a canoe on a clear night.

Since Lookout Rock and the Stone Throne face each other, my theory is that over the millennia, people have sometimes stood or sat in the two locations and communicated. A scout would be able to easily see any paddlers entering the area. If they wanted to, they could then quickly relay this, or other messages, down to a person in the Stone Throne, who might then pass along the information to people in the campsite area.

Although standing on the high lookout affects people in different ways, including vertigo and fear in some, for me it awakens something joyful in my spirit. The place is inspiring. It feels mystical and sacred, and is conducive to wonder and deep thinking. Surely many have felt powerful emotions there, perhaps even had revelations, visions or, or at the very least, used metaphors, such as calling it an eagle's perch, or a giant pulpit. One can see back up the river to places gone by, all the way past the Cedars campsite, to near where the water flows in, almost a kilometre away, after the last small set of Natch Rapids. Leaving the top of Lookout Rock and carefully walking a couple hundred metres downriver along the edge of the

5 *Barron Canyon Trail – History of the Canyon*, Published by "The Friends of Algonquin Park, P.O. Box 248, Whitney, ON K0J 2M0, www.algonquinpark.on.ca In cooperation with Ontario Parks. ISBN 1-895709-75-x 2014

clifftops, there are more spectacular views of the canyon – the journey still to come.

On my lucky 7-11 arrival day, I was especially thankful to have another opportunity to sit in the Stone Throne, on the lower of the two cliffs. Another big revolution had come all the way around. It was a new summer, a new year. I intended to later hike up the steep rough trail to visit Lookout Rock. But for the time being I was simply at peace, content to gaze around, let everything soak in, and take stock of my feelings. I was happy, satisfied, and understood more than ever that I have been so very fortunate in my life. My spirit felt restored and whole. Remnants of difficulties and wounds from the past seemed healed, even irrelevant.

With a smile, I thought how rare it was, in this often difficult and constantly-changing life, that I ever got to feel this good. Still, I hadn't forgotten that only a couple of kilometres upriver, I had come far too close to dying. My life could have been much shorter.

I thought of a few lines from a poem I had written many years earlier, sitting beside another very special river, the Dumoine, in Quebec. It is titled, "At the End of the Portage," and the last few lines say:

> *So I'd best look around*
> *Soak it up while I can*
> *Changes will come,*
> *Rivers run, rivers ran.*
> *At the end of this portage*
> *My ready boat waits.*[6]

---

6 The complete "At the End of the Portage" poem is located at the end of this book.

I stayed quiet a little while longer, as the scent of pine and cedar breathed fresh life into the air and into me. And as I sat in my blissful reverie, casually looking around, I was thrilled to witness a rare treat. Three eagles soared high over the cliff tops, almost directly above Lookout Rock. With their extremely wide and flat wingspans, these very large birds were surely not vultures, nor any other kind of hawk. I watched them for about ten minutes as they glided, slowly wheeling, gradually kettling upwards. Eventually, they rose so high that they almost disappeared. Finally, only visible as tiny specks, they slowly cruised off, loosely together, heading downriver. I glowed and thought "Meegwetch."

Besides being reminded of my recent sighting of two eagles above Lake Travers, my mind flashed way back, to another memorable eagle, one that had kettled directly above our group on that Mountain River trip all those years ago. It had appeared just moments before we finally recovered the pinned canoe from the river. After hauling the flattened boat out, and repairing it, our group named that location "Eagle Rock," because of our very special, timely visitor. That eagle too, had left by gilding off downriver.

And as I watched those three Petawawa River eagles gradually drift away, high above the waters to come, I smiled, and thought of my three wonderful children.

End of the Portage

14

Back in the tent, to try for a third time to rest a bit, I left both screen doors wide open, attempting to limit the heat. It was too hot for any bugs. Using my big canoe pack as a back pillow, I sat and wrote in my journal, catching up. I had just finished the part about seeing the eagles when I heard voices: more visitors.

In the afternoon stillness, I easily overheard a man and woman talking with Nelson, and assumed it was the newly-weds. By the time I had crawled out of my tent, zipped the doors, and headed over to the water's edge, Nelson had told them briefly about me. He mentioned my canoe wreck on Rollway last year, and that I was currently on a return trip. He also told them he was sure I would share the big campsite with them. At that moment, I stepped down onto the shore beside my canoe.

Now I could see them, over to my right, upriver, only twenty metres away. The young couple sat relaxed with their knees up, floating in their red canoe only about five metres offshore. They had nestled their boat in snugly, right beside the upstream edge of the semi-floating jam. This was as close as they could get to Nelson, who was standing near his tent. I called out a friendly greeting and waved, and Nelson said, "That's the guy I told you about." He briefly introduced Todd and Lindsay to me, and they flashed big smiles and waved back. I told them they were very welcome to join me, and that the site was quite big. There was lots of room. They cheerfully accepted.

That's when something truly astonishing happened. At that precise place and time, for some reason the man in the stern looked down into the water, under the side of their boat. When I remember this scene, I see it in ultra slow-motion, almost stop-motion, with an over-exposed sky, and a wonderful kind of electricity flowing through me and the air all around us. Looking back up, and directly at me, we locked eyes and he said, "I think I see a boat, under the water. Right here!"

Suddenly riveted, I listened intently as he went on to say that it was kind of hard to see, and seemed in really rough shape, and was lying on its side, about a metre below the surface. But it did look like a canoe. I was dumbfounded. Before I could spit out the same words, Nelson had already asked him, 'What colour is it?' After another quick look, Todd looked a me and replied, 'Red!'

My heart surged with a hope I had thought was lost forever. Stunned with disbelief, I asked, "Does it have wood gunwales?" The young man peered back down into the water, and seemed to pause and think for a moment. Then he called back, "It doesn't look like it has hardly any gunwales at all. But what's left, are wood."

I knew in that instant: This was my boat!

Almost bursting with excitement, in five minutes I had quickly welcomed Todd and Lindsay ashore at my campsite, and pulled their new red boat up beside mine. Unable to contain myself a moment longer, I grabbed my paddle and rocket-launched my canoe. My mind spinning, I dashed over to take a look. How could it be?

And on this day of so many coincidences, another one now occurred. At the same moment that I sped across the short span of water, a couple in one of the mango-coloured canoes paddled out from the Cedars campsite, probably to head over and look at the cliffs. As I got half-way to my destination, their boat happened to be positioned perfectly, only a few metres away from the raft of trees and branches. Without hesitation, I detoured slightly, paddled right up to them, pulled my digital camera out of my pocket, and handed it to the woman in the bow. Despite her confused expression, I urged her to please take pictures, lots of pictures, of what was about to happen. With no further explanation to the puzzled strangers, and now with two people on the water plus three on land watching the unfolding scene, I did a few more strong power strokes directly toward the place where the couple had been floating. In seconds my new canoe was sitting above the spot.

Staring deep into the water, it only took a moment for any remaining doubt to disappear. It doesn't take much to recognize an old friend. I was looking at one end of what was left of my boat. The water above it was about a metre deep, but there was no question. With submerged branches, above, inside, and surrounding it, I saw part of the familiar hull, positioned on edge, its open mouth facing up-river. It had become incorporated into the raft's assemblage of tree trunks, branches and grasses, and appeared well along the way to becoming part of a dam. I could dimly see one end of the canoe, and it had a couple of still-attached pieces of wood gunwales. This wasn't just any boat. It was *my* boat! And there it lay, only twenty metres (65 feet) from my tent, right beside the big Natch Cliffs campsite!

I gently pushed on it with the blade of my paddle, and was surprised to see it sink a bit, then bob slowly back up, stopping again roughly a metre from the surface. It never did touch bottom. Although packed full of mud and branches, and lying on its side, it was semi-floating. When I pushed with my other hand on the nearest big tree trunk log of the jam, it too, and most of the large raft, seemed to move and bob slightly. Although anchored to shore, the entire thing was floating!

I had wrecked this boat the previous year, in August of 2005, half way down Rollway, at kilometre 62.5. Now, there it was, in July of 2006, almost a full year later, and the boat was resting at kilometre 64.5, two full kilometres further along the river. Somehow, over eleven months, it had travelled down the rest of Rollway Rapids, gone through a long section of flat-water, the two full sets of Natch Rapids, plus the last small set that spills into this lake-like section. Then it had continued to move a further half-kilometre along the edge of the calm, wide section of the river by the two campsites. Finally, it had come to rest – and who knows how long ago – only five metres offshore, on river-left, a metre below the surface, at the edge of this old raft of fallen trees, branches, grasses and flotsam. It seemed miraculous.

Besides finding the canoe in the first place, I was stunned that my old friend had come to rest at this exact spot, by the very campsite we had been trying to reach on that difficult day! Like some legendary injured horse with no rider, she had found her way to the stable, to our destination. And there she had stayed, as if waiting, until this special day. 7-11 indeed!

Expressions like, "What are the odds!" and "Unbelievable!" were inadequate to express my wonder. I was totally flabbergasted. But I didn't need to think for more than a moment. I knew exactly what I had to do. I would get her out of the river.

Kneeling in my new canoe, I slowly reached my right arm down into the water until my armpit was wet. I couldn't see the Mad River Explorer bow logo, with the little bunny on it, and so figured this must be the stern. With immense satisfaction, I saw that the thick blue, semi-circle grab-handle rope I had installed so many years ago, was still there. Tied to it was an extremely tattered bit of snapped floatable yellow painter line. I poked the end of the ABS once more, directly with my fingertips this time, and watched as it again bobbed down, then rose slowly back up.

Slipping my fingers inside the tip of the stern, I raised it slightly until I could get my full hand underneath and really grab it. Lifting slowly, my fingers were able to slide back and reach the grab-handle, and firmly haul. This made the end, and what appeared to be the entire hull, start to rise. As my battered canoe neared the surface, I could see that it was jammed full with small logs, branches and black muck. This was why it felt so heavy. As soon as I could, I reached inside with my other hand and began scooping everything out. It took only a few minutes to dig and flush most of the mucky contents out that had probably taken the river, and perhaps some furry helpers, months to pack in. Eventually all that was left were hundreds of green and black fibrous stains on the plastic, left by the roots of aquatic plants that had apparently tried to anchor themselves and grow on this strange host.

Some of the tears and cuts in the ABS were so long that when I moved it, the whole hull bent like a folding hinge. I knew firsthand how hard it was to try and cut through that stuff, let alone tear it like that, as if it were a piece of taffy or cardboard. I looked for the spot where I had tried to saw down into her last year, and found it right away. Nature had completed my job and then some.

Besides the old saw cut, there was a complete break where the ABS plastic had cracked or snapped, only about 40 centimetres further along, parallel to my effort. Another diagonal, wavy twisted tear below these two openings created a section that had become an almost detached piece of plastic, one that was still connected to the hull by only a small remnant shred of ABS. The forces needed to mutilate the thick, tough layered plastic like that must have been tremendous.

I reached out to hold this loose section, and to my wonder, it came off right in my hand! Eleven months in the river, and the part I had sawed into came off, at that exact second, in my hand! If it had separated on its own from the main hull, and fallen off at any earlier moment, it would have been washed away and lost, and probably lie buried in river mud somewhere. But there in my hand, I stared at that red piece of my old boat, and saw that it said, in big white letters, "Mad." It was the first part from the decal in the middle of the boat that said "Mad River Canoe." I pitched it into the bottom of my boat and went back to work.

Usually, when a canoe is overturned and another one is nearby and able to help, the most common rescue method is the "canoe-over-canoe" maneuver. With the swimming paddlers holding the tips of the rescue boat, one end of the upside-down canoe is tilted and rolled slightly sideways, to break the suction, then lifted upwards out of the water and pulled across the gunwales in front of the rescuing person in the stern. The rest of the upside-down canoe is then quickly slid out of the water, forming a "t" or a cross, as it rests on the rescue boat. It sits there for a minute or so and drains, and once empty is rolled forward on the rescuer's gunwales, away from the stern, until sitting upright. It's then slid back into the water, good as new. With the rescuer holding the newly-righted boat steady, the swimmers climb back in, and paddle on.

The battered old hull that I was trying to haul out of the Petawawa, wasn't a perfect candidate for this type of rescue. It resembled a half-torn banana peel more than a canoe. But it was worth a try.

Once the contents had been had been completely flushed, I slowly hauled what was left of my old canoe upside down, right out of the water, and plunked it like a huge, floppy fish, perpendicular across the wood gunwales of my new Mad River. After four seasons in the Petawawa, she had come back above the surface. Once drained, I rolled her upright and took a good look inside. With no remaining seats or thwarts, hardly any gunwales, many cuts, tears and creases, and hundreds of spider-webbed traces of things that had tried to grow, she was not the boat she had once been. Exposed to the fresh summer air once more, she was a broken shell. But she had risen.

Aware that those cuts and breaks would quickly make her fill up with water again, I nevertheless gently slid her back into the river, hoping the ABS would at least provide enough buoyancy that I would be able to tow her over to my camp. I tied the end of my throwbag rope to the blue grab handle, and after letting out a few metres, clipped the rope with a carabiner to the stern thwart of my new boat.

On my way past the couple in their mango canoe, the woman handed my camera back and said she had taken lots of pictures. I thanked her profusely, and took a few more, looking back at my prize in tow. A bathtub full of water would have had more freeboard. I carefully landed my new boat by the campsite, stepped out, and pulled my old boat part way onto shore. We had finally made it.

While I was on the water, Lindsay and Todd, who were obviously experienced campers, had quickly and efficiently unloaded and moved their canoe so it wouldn't be in my way, and set up their tent. They greeted me home like a conquering hero, and took several more pictures, this time with me posing proudly, holding the Mad piece in front of me like a sign, standing by my two red Mad Rivers. It was a time of great joy and wonder.

After the photo shoot, I drained the old boat and hauled it ten metres from the water's edge to the far end of the large clearing, near my tent. Although it was now only a ripped, cut, bent, ABS hull, covered with dents, abrasions, slime, and traces of roots, it was such a marvelous sight to see it on land!

There was hardly any wood left, except a few short broken sections of gunwales. Six of the eight blue sponges that I had glued to the floor with contact cement, as built-in knee pads many years ago, had been ripped out. Only the glue remained. Of the eight seat blocks and metal bolts, all but two were gone. The two still in place were bent. Only the pairs of small D-rings that I had glued to the inside of each end, to hold in the now-absent airbags, had stayed solidly in place. There was that single strong blue grab handle still functional on the stern, with its attached bit of tattered yellow painter. But the one on the bow was gone. I counted a total of eight major cuts in the plastic, and several places where sections of the ABS had been deformed, as if stretched, melted, ripped or crumpled. She had surely been through a lot.

Yet with very little internal debate, my mind quickly switched from damage assessment to considering possible repairs, patches, improvised thwarts, whatever might be done, to make this old hull float again, at least for a little while. I wanted, if possible, to try and bring her home. After a celebration supper, and more shared tripping stories with my three new river friends, I went to work.

As my group of eight had done fifteen years earlier on the Mountain River, I improvised. Attempting to regain and hold some of the canoe's lost shape, I used whatever was at hand, mainly branches, string and ropes, to create a rough frame of cedar-branch gunwales. Out of thin logs, I also made and tied in, a makeshift centre thwart and two end thwarts.

Once this frame was "complete," and a few photographs taken, I stopped for a break, and got into my new Mad River, which had been left waiting by the shore. Paddling a short distance over to the base of the cliffs, I gathered a boatful of dry firewood. Todd and Lindsay also went out in their canoe, and got more wood, so we would be all set for the evening and also breakfast.

I had noticed when I first arrived at the campsite that, perhaps for safety reasons, some person or group had moved the location of the site's fire circle. It was now about eight metres (26 feet) away from the place where I had seen it on other trips, the spot which I thought of as its historic location. The large circle of stones was now in the centre of the main clearing, allowing bigger groups to sit around it. The "original" bed of the fire, had been right behind the large rock outcropping beside the water, the one where I had sat relaxing just before my swim, flanked by two giant pine sentries. That whiskey jack had landed on the exact spot that had previously been the fire bed. Todd and Lindsay had chosen this splendid location, with its premier views of the cliffs and the river, to locate their tent. What a special place to sleep.

Nelson built us a big bonfire. I sat and enjoyed it for twenty minutes, and then went back to work. Using one of my old T-shirts, I started wiping the hull down, gradually removing the slime, dirt, and fibrous growths, from both inside and out. When the shirt got filthy I would rinse it, wring it out, warm it over the fire again, then repeat the process. I did this roughly fifteen times. Knowing duct tape won't stick to anything moist or dirty, I eventually cleaned, dried, and warmed the entire hull.

Next, a rough patching job began. The kit bag in my canoe pack had a lot of string, ropes, and miscellaneous repair items, but I had forgotten my roll of duct tape. It had accidentally gone back to Ottawa in the trunk of Jill's car. Generously, Todd and Lindsay gave me their own medium-sized roll. Once the old boat was more or less clean, braced with branches, tied together, warmed and dried, I patched its holes and cracks the best I could, using their entire roll. I knew there would be very little strength or staying power in this flimsy craft, but hoped she would at least be floatable in the morning, when I would try my best to tow her the rest of the way down the river to McManus Lake, and then drive her home.

Finally, after three hours' work, we covered it for the night with my small orange nylon tarp, to keep out any possible rain, since the hull wasn't structurally sound enough be turned upside down. It now looked a little more like a boat than when it was dragged out of the river, and also resembled a big orange cocoon, or a chrysalis. Metamorphosis again. Then it was time to relax with stories around the fire, until bed at 11:00.

Over the course of the evening we each relayed several more of our personal adventures. I told them about finding that piece of moose spine at this exact campsite many years ago, and of the laughs we had after its later return to the river. I also shared more details of my wreck of the previous summer, and the saga of our canoe on the Mountain River fifteen years earlier, which our group had dubbed "The Mary Ellen Carter the Second." I even sang a couple of verses of that great Stan Rogers song. We laughed and marvelled at the long list of coincidences, connections, and blessings that had somehow come together on this very lucky day – coincidences that had led to me finding my lost boat. Or maybe it had found me.

I snuggled into my sleeping bag, exhausted, but still amazed. As I drifted off, besides my mind replaying the surreal vision of looking deep into the water and seeing my old canoe, I thought of those three eagles, and of the morning's dazzling flurry of little butterflies.

End of the Portage

15

Life felt very good that night, but my mind was busy. I slept only a little, working through various scenarios, counting lemons. Pulling and trying to steer a lame-duck empty boat through rapids wouldn't be easy. I knew that the chance of a successful outcome would be low, but only for a few minutes did I wonder why I wanted to do it. My gut told me loud and clear I had to at least try to get my old boat home. Even if it didn't work out. And that was exactly what I would do: try. But I also reminded myself of my promise to Jill, to keep safe. I would cut the tow rope and ditch the wrecked boat in an instant if things got too dangerous.

A couple of times I rolled over and looked through the screen door at the canoe. It was still there. There was no rain, or even a breeze. As if in a dream, or a giant epic painting by one of the old masters, the black silhouettes of the silent surrounding pines seemed to stand guard. The whole scene was back-dropped by the cliffs and lit by the dim glow from the night sky above. There was no sound. Timeless.

Because the sun rises behind the shadow of the big cliffs, daybreak always happens slower than usual at this campsite. It takes at least an extra half-hour for the light to get high enough to finally appear over the top of the Lookout Rock cliff. Normally it's a great place for relaxing and sleeping-in, but I had much to do. At first light I got up, ready to finish a few further repairs, pack, and get paddling.

In the night, I had decided that it would be a good plan to wrap my old boat tightly in the orange nylon tarp, like the skin of a drum. Although the material was thin, at least it was waterproof. I could wrap almost the entire hull, using several strings to tie it securely. Hopefully it would gird the structure a bit, helping hold its shape, while also keeping the water out. On the down side, it wouldn't offer a lot protection, since it would easily tear if grazed against rocks. But it only cost me thirty dollars, and could easily be replaced. At least it would be something. As soon as they got up I told Lindsay and Todd of my plan, and we all laughed when they told me that the two of them had thought of the exact same idea in the night. Right after breakfast we would go to work.

When Nelson woke, he quickly packed up his gear and tent, ready to leave, then joined us as we relaxed around the breakfast fire. He described how, after this Petawawa River section of his trip, he was going to go on and paddle some of the big stuff on the Ottawa. Todd and Lindsay, besides being currently on their honeymoon, were both teachers on their summer holidays. They told us they had both also recently been whitewater paddling instructors. We shared a lot in common, not just because of our shared love of nature and canoeing, but also because Jill and I are both teachers as well. We've experienced the honour and many joys and trials of teaching, plus the priceless bonus of having every summer off together. Thirty-four years earlier, we too had been married on a beautiful July day, and for part of our own honeymoon, had also canoed and camped in Algonquin Park.

Over coffee, we all talked more about Outdoor Education, and how very important it is for every child to have several first-hand experiences in natural areas, as part of their basic education. I tried to explain, probably unconvincingly, that I really didn't wreck boats often, and in fact had rarely experienced any difficult paddling incidents – and never one with students on any school trip.

Todd and I discussed trends in repair kits for boat emergencies. We eventually decided that perhaps all that is really needed, for a quick temporary repair kit with these plastic boats, is a spool of strong thin aluminum wire, plus a spike to poke holes for threading. And of course, lots of duct tape.

Nelson and I continued to chat about our Mountain River trips, and the exciting end-of-the-trip shuttle motor boat ride our groups had both enjoyed going back up the swollen Mackenzie River to our starting point at Norman Wells with Frank Pope, our mutual outfitter. Nelson joked about being frightened by a black bear he saw swimming straight towards them in the Mackenzie, near town. It turned out to be a friendly local dog.

Sitting around the fire, Nelson discretely made a very kind offer. He said he would be fine to wait and paddle out with me that day, and help me along my way. What a nice guy. I knew my trip would take many more hours than his solo, plus I would likely need to stop often, and quite possibly have to camp again somewhere. My progress would probably be slow, and the situation might get dangerous at times. I didn't want to slow Nelson down or risk his safety. Besides, this was a task I felt I needed to do alone. With sincere thanks, I declined. We both agreed that paddling solo, the way we both enjoy so much, is never really lonely. You always run into such great people. This proves true time and time again.

We tidied up from breakfast, then the four of us worked together, finishing a few more adjustments. When we had gotten her as shipshape as we could, we tied the tarp on tight. At about 11:30, using the timer on my camera, the four of us crouched for smiling group-portrait shots beside the fully bundled "repaired" boat.

Having already done his pack-up, Nelson then loaded his canoe, and with the three of us wishing him safe journey, pushed off from shore. Passing by the giant cliff with Lookout Rock perched high above, he soon reached the last corner visible from the big campsite, where there is a massive wedge-shaped chunk of rock that looks as if it is pointing up. Long ago it probably cracked away from the main precipice. After returning our final waves, he took a couple more strokes and was gone.

A few small sparklers and a little bag of Swedish Berries candies were all I could give to Lindsay and Todd. I wanted to somehow thank them for discovering my boat, their many kindnesses, and for their indispensable duct tape. The tasty berries had come as part of my staple of candies in the blue barrel. But the sealed package of sparklers had been in my day-pack for years, left over from some forgotten Outdoor Education school trip long ago. It hadn't even fallen out when that same pack, now secured with dependable locking twist ties on its zippers, spilled open and spewed most of its contents into the river. This unusual gift caused Lindsay to laugh with glee and comment, "You certainly are a teacher! Why do you have sparklers with you?" My answer was obvious. "You never know when you might need some sparklers."

The three of us gently lifted the shrouded boat down to the water's edge, and took more pictures. We shared big smiles when we saw that it floated in the shallows. I again told them how great it was to have met them, and also that the two of them were both teachers. I wished them a happy honeymoon, many happy summer holidays, and thanked them one more time for finding my boat. We traded email addresses and hugged.

Earlier, I had told them about the Stone Throne. By the time I was set to go, they had already been over to check it out. They said they would probably also hike up to Lookout Rock later. By then I would of course be long gone with my two canoes, and they would be alone. The mango boat family had left earlier, shortly before Nelson left, and the paddlers that had run Rollway the day before while I stood by, hadn't been seen since then. They must have camped upriver at one of the other Natch campsites, before they even got to the Big Cliffs area. For Todd and Lindsay, the river and this special Big Cliffs campsite, would probably be all theirs that night.

Shortly after noon, everything was loaded and ready. I burned a bit of sweetgrass, gently eased my strange, two-part rig away from shore, and started paddling. As I left, Todd and Lindsay were very happy, and camped in paradise. They took more pictures as I went past the cliffs, and later shared them with me via email.

To pull the big orange barge behind, I used a floating painter rope clipped to my centre yoke, adjusted so that it was roughly two metres long. I was prepared to release it in a flash if hazards developed. Delighted to have begun my journey homeward, I was also relieved to see the old boat floated quite high in the water, like a big balloon.

I passed by the base of the cliff that has Lookout Rock on top, and said to myself, "I'll check it out next time." Then as my long, articulated rig approached the corner with the wedge-shaped rock, I turned my canoe slightly so I could take my last look upstream, to the places gone by. I saw Lindsay sitting in the Stone Throne, with Todd standing right beside her. They were both smiling, enthusiastically waving goodbye. What a vision to remember.

The river floated me around the corner, and I was alone again. With a slight headwind, I paddled slowly away, into yet another beautiful summer day.

16

My confidence was strong, and the weather and water conditions excellent. I was determined to keep vigilant and not wipe out, ready to let go of the towed boat and give up on the mission at any time. If it ultimately became unavoidable, I would indeed just leave her. Perhaps, despite all my efforts, what remained of my old boat would end up being dragged into the forest somewhere along the way, and buried under leaves and branches. But first I would give it a good try.

Before I arrived at the Big Cliffs site, my solo paddling had only needed to propel myself, my gear, and my canoe. Now I also hauled a second load, and everything moved slowly at first like a freight train gradually getting rolling. My mind played with metaphors. That thing I was hauling back there was like an albatross, a lame horse, a big potentially dangerous orange Portuguese man-of-war, a pup trailer, perhaps even a battering ram. But we were on our way home.

I settled into a steady rhythm: paddle, paddle, paddle, feel the backwards tug, watch the barge catch up a bit, then repeat the pattern. It was slow going but the albatross was still floating high. It looked like there was little or no water going in. Paddling the 2.5 kilometres of calm, flatwater to the first swift took a full hour. Normally it would take me half that. I knew then for certain that this was going to be a very long day. I had a total of 24.5 kilometres to travel, to reach the far end of McManus Lake.

Navigating my train through the first swift was easy, but demonstrated what I would be up against in the longer, more difficult rapids coming up. The lighter old boat kept wanting to glide forward sideways, and almost pass my loaded canoe. To keep it safely behind, I had to paddle hard in spurts that were quite a bit quicker than I wanted to. This would then snap it back into line, but the pace was difficult to maintain, and sometimes sent me flying along.

In the flat section below the swift, I removed the carabi-neer used to clip the tow line to the centre yoke, and switched to simply sitting on the loose end of the rope. This was much safer, because in a difficult situation I could quickly just shift the weight off my bum, and instantly let the towed boat go. I was aware of the likely risks involved in navigating the coming long sets of rapids with two linked 16 foot canoes. There was a potential to lose control of what might become an unwieldy 12 metre (38 foot) moving structure. One or both canoes, or the tow rope itself, might snag, and become hung up on some obstacle, causing both boats to wreck. I steeled my resolve, ready to release the rope.

My average flatwater cruising speed seemed to be about two kilometres an hour. At the end of the next kilometre I floated quickly through a second swift, and soon after noticed the towed boat was tugging a little harder than it had before. I knew what that meant. Some water had gotten in, and was beginning to weigh it down. I had heard a couple of small bumps back there as I tried to guide both boats safely through, but steering from remote involves considerable delays and unresponsiveness. I knew it wouldn't take much to rip that thin nylon skin wide open. The process had probably already started.

Soon I was only half a kilometre upriver from the start of Schooner Rapids. Normally this four kilometre long ride through Class 1 and 2 whitewater is a delight. It sweeps along quickly and continuously with only one short break just past half way, where it a widens for half a kilometre into a small lake. Preparing for the workout, I had a drink of water and a handful of gorp, and took a few minutes to rest. Trying to get a quicker response time to my steering efforts, I also choked up a bit more on the towrope. Now there was only about a metre and a half left between boats. The music didn't play this time. I was too worried.

Then the whole rig slipped over the brink. In seconds, we were flying through big splashes and lots of rocks. Despite my best efforts, I had no ability to slow things down. The old boat unavoidably grazed off a few boulders during the first kilometre and began riding lower. As feared, at one point the floating rope between boats became snagged on a rock. While back-paddling furiously to try and take the strain off the caught line, I watched with dismay as the heavy orange trailer swung sideways to the right, then pendulumed all the way down, until it was floating only a metre away, beside me, held by the tight rope, aiming backward. Thinking this was surely the end, I shifted my butt, and released the line.

By some grace, this resulted in instantly unsnagging the rope. I grabbed the end just as it was about to spew over the stern and be lost to the river. But that slackening of the rope also allowed the orange boat that needed to be behind me, to continue drifting up ahead. I could see she was riding very low, and knew there must be quite a ballast of water in there.

With more frantic paddling and rock-dodging I managed to power my new canoe out in front again, while also getting it over to river-left a little. But, although the towed boat was now behind, it floated broadside to the current, and was lumbering along like a big log. Everything was still barrelling down rock-studded Schooner full tilt, and the old boat's sudden jerks and lurches were tell-tale signs of several scrapes and hits off rocks and the bottom. We wouldn't make it like this.

With several more power strokes and hard yanks on the rope, I managed to haul everything over toward a low shallow section of shore on river-left, just after flying past a campsite. I eddied the whole rig out. We had made it past the river's first big zigzag bend to the left.

Jumping into the shallows, I gently hauled both boats part way up on the loose rocks. Once they were secure, I looked inside the old canoe through a small opening I had left in the top of the tarp to allow for bailing. The hull was three quarters full of water. It looked almost as swamped as it had been when I first towed it out of the river! Grudgingly pleased to have at least made it through the first kilometre of Schooner, the reality was that my mission was now highly unsafe – probably impossible.

I scrabbled about aimlessly on the stones. It was almost 3:00. In the 30-degree afternoon sun I was shaky, almost dizzy. It had taken over two-and-a-half hours of difficult, risky work to travel just 5 kilometres. There were still 20 kilometres to go, including the second half of Schooner Rapids and all of Five Mile Rapids. I knew I couldn't do it. Forced to abandon my old wrecked boat on Rollway last year, I would have to leave it again.

While wrestling with this difficult thought, I watched as the two couples from Rollway paddled past me over on river-right. Cruising their canoes easily around the sweeping bend, they waved cheerfully as they continued down the rest of Schooner. They had no idea of my situation. Maybe they were able to quickly put the scene together in some way, and deduce that I had found my old canoe and was taking it home. I suppose to them that orange cocoon looked pretty sound. But I knew better.

Updating my options, they were now extremely few. I could ditch what was left of the old boat, right then and there, or perhaps somehow get it back up around the corner to the campsite I had just passed. Or maybe I should just drag it off into the woods and leave it there, as I had imagined someone had done last year. Who knows, sometime in the future I might come back to the spot with friends and retrieve it. But even as this thought whizzed through my mind, I knew it would never happen. I shook my head and told myself, "When something is over, it should just be over." It would be best to just say my goodbyes and abandon this liability once and for all.

My self-criticism and wavering ran deep. Why was it so hard for me to let go? Why had I even returned to this river? Probably I should have left that carcass where I found it, let her rest in peace, packed full of muck and branches. The river had put her there. I should have respected that. It was disrespectful to move her, misguided to attempt to patch her, and stupid to think I could bring her home. How could I possibly do it? That last stretch had been off the scale dangerous. I had promises to keep, to be safe. I tried listening to the river, but heard no counsel.

I went over to my new boat and dug into the barrel. After grabbing a little food, I rested on a boulder, ate slowly, and drank from my water bottle. My focus soon changed to the lovely tinkling call-and-response songs of two birds that were talking to each other somewhere deep in the forest. I had heard their calls before. Then my gaze turned to a few small flowers blooming their hearts out, near the water's edge. The sky shone deep blue with only a few dazzlingly bright, white little clouds. Lines from the old Max Ehrmann poem *Desiderata* drifted through my mind:

> *With all its sham, drudgery, and broken dreams,*
> *it is still a beautiful world.*
> *Be cheerful. Strive to be happy.*[7]

Yes indeed, life is good. And it goes on all around us, all the time. I also thought of another line from my own old poem, "*At The End of the Portage,*"

> *And the river, the river,*
> *Always passing by and nigh.*

Memory tapes started playing in my mind, of previous trips when I had paddled these beautiful rapids with ease. I remembered that at the lower end of this first half of Schooner, the river is crossed by a broad hydro corridor of tall, high voltage towers and wires. In my hazy mind's eye, I also saw a small old bridge crossing the river at that point. A bridge! Yes, there was a bridge! Where there's a bridge, there is usually a road! Grabbing my map, I confirmed the hydro corridor was about one-and-a-half kilometres further down the present continuous stretch of whitewater, just at the point where the river

---

7 *Desiderata* was written by Max Ehrmann in 1927, and was first published in 1948. Ehrmann, Bertha, ed. (1948). The Poems of Max Ehrmann, Bruce Humphries, Inc. p. 165. Original Text www.desiderata.com

begins to widen for a short time into the small lake. The bridge that I remembered was for a small service road that skirts the edge of the hydro corridor. A road! What if I could just get to that road?

A new option arose: bail like crazy and get this orange albatross to float long enough to travel through only 1.5 more kilometres of whitewater without a crisis. Once under the old bridge I could haul it out on the river-right shore by the beginning of the power corridor, where the map showed a little campsite. If I could accomplish that, the most dangerous and difficult part of my task would be done. I could leave it there, beside the service road.

Without having a wreck to tow any more, I would then be able to paddle the rest of my trip unencumbered, camp at the end of McManus Lake that night as planned, and the next morning drive to the park staff building, which would be only 20 minutes away at Achray. Hopefully the wardens there would allow me to drive down the rough service road to retrieve my old boat. Failing that, my fallback was that it would just be left there permanently, out of the river. But I wasn't ready to accept that yet.

It seemed like a wild idea, but then the whole retrieval process had been crazy. This was much safer than trying to paddle the entire distance while pulling an unwieldy pup-trailer, and quite a bit less work. I wouldn't have to say goodbye just yet, and would only need to get through a kilometre and a half in one piece. I started bailing.

As expected, there were several holes in the tarp. Even shovelling water out as fast as I could, the river leaked straight back in. Once on the water, I wouldn't have long. After giving up on the bailing, I would have to jump into my new canoe, and get the heck going quickly if I hoped to make it downriver before the wreck sank completely, got pinned, or snagged on the bottom like an anchor.

I readied everything and pushed off. Within 100 metres, I could see that it was already beginning to sink. By the end of the first half-kilometre, it had become a two thirds submerged submarine, repeatedly bumping and scraping along rocks and on the bottom. With lots of strong yanking and furious paddling, I was just barely able to keep it from pinning as we barrelled along. I knew there was very little strength left in her. Twice I almost released the rope.

With about half a kilometre left, I looked back and saw she had rolled completely upside down, and was now being dragged along belly up. Everything but a few centimetres on my end were below the surface. Steering the best I could, while keeping my own boat out of its way and avoiding rocks, we somehow made it through the gauntlet. The two boats sailed one behind the other, under the finish line of the bridge.

I gradually slowed the whole rig down and, doing an extended whiplash eddy turn, navigated over to river-right. Hopping out once again into the shallows, I dragged the two boats to the calm outwash water beside the little campsite, then pulled them part way onto the shore. It was 3:45. I had traveled 7 kilometres in three and a half hours and was exhausted, but tremendously happy.

After carefully peeling the orange skin off of the wreck, I used a big pine tree's branches to hang it up and examine it. The bright sunlight shining through in several places confirmed it was full of rips and tears, both big and small, especially in the middle. I thought for a moment that possibly the tarp could be patched in the future. But probably not. Best to just chuck it. Let it go. I would buy a new one. Still, it was a kind of trophy. I took pictures and brought it with me as a souvenir.

By bailing, carefully tipping, and gently pulling the old boat further onto higher dry land, I got the last of the water out of her. I dragged it through the campsite, to rest beside the edge of the bush road, near the place where it crosses the Petawawa River via the old bridge. I knew this would be her last time in any river.

I left the old canoe resting upside down, to wait for a motorized ride. It felt quite a lot better than abandonment. I knew exactly where she was: out of the water, resting beside a road, ready for the next leg of the journey.

Before climbing back in my new boat, I walked half way across the old bridge and stood watching the oncoming flow of the river for a while. Staring at the rock-studded Class 2 rapids that my boats had just passed through, I was grateful to have somehow been kept safe. The river had once again been good to me. I was also very thankful that I would never have to do that again! Water under the bridge! I took out the sweetgrass and burned a bit. Meegwetch.

Feeling tired but elated, just after 4:00, I set off again to paddle the last eighteen kilometres. My aim was to make camp at the far end of McManus before dark. Without the drag from the old boat, my canoe felt light as a feather, and flew along. The journey once again became a pleasant meditative solo. The flatwater sections were quick to cross, and the rapids a joy to navigate. The boat never took in a single splash.

Lindsay and Todd had traded campsite paperwork with me when we parted. I gave them my official booking at the Big Cliffs campsite. They gave me theirs on Smith Lake, in case it was needed. I hoped to not have to take them up on it. Along the way I passed two camps. One had the two Rollway couples, who again waved at me, and may have wondered where my orange towed boat had gone. The other site had the mango boats family settled in for the night. Nelson was long gone.

The light headwind of the afternoon dropped to a flat calm by early evening, helping speed my progress. At 8:00 pm, after four hours of steady strong paddling, I pulled my canoe onto the beach in front of a little campsite by the McManus Lake take-out. Like Lake Travers, McManus is a large widening of the Petawawa River, and with no wind to cause even a ripple, it was calm as can be, a perfect giant mirror. The spot where I landed was only a five-minute walk to the parking area where Jill and I had left the car.

I had finished, safe and sound. My thoughts drifted upriver to the old boat. It wasn't so sound of course, but at least it was out of the river. I knew where it was, just back up there a little way. My head continued to grapple with the multiple coincidences that had converged to bring all this about.

I set up a quick camp and ate supper, then walked back down to the beach and took my last few photographs of the glassy shining surface of the lake, as it reflected the blazing summer sunset over my beached, beautiful, new canoe.

After a quick swim, I crashed in the tent, exhausted. In the morning, my gear would be piled into the car, and my new boat tied on the roof. Then I would drive to Achray on Grand Lake and talk with any staff I could find.

It felt so good to get flat on my back. This time I saw no little butterflies, no silhouettes of giant pines backed by cliffs. I heard no sounds of coming storms, no rapids, no whispered counsel. Everything was just calm, still, peaceful. I closed my eyes and nodded off to the soothing sound of a whip-poor-will repeatedly calling its name somewhere near the tent: "Whip-poor-will, Whip-poor-will, Whip-poor-will."

17

I woke with the first glow of dawn once again, but this time, without the deep shadow of the big cliffs, it happened earlier, just after 5:00. The Achray office wouldn't be open for hours, so I allowed myself the luxury of staying in bed relaxing, enjoying the start of another fabulous day. I thought of hugging Jill and telling her everything.

Looking through the door screen, I watched the morning mist begin to lift slowly here and there over the sleeping lake. Hints of a coming blue sky poked through in a few high places. It was going to be lovely. With no rain, and little or no wind, it would be perfect for transporting two boats home on the car. Twilight slowly brightened to full daylight, while all the time my little friend, the whip-poor-will, who had served as my alarm clock, cooed over and over all around the tent. Perhaps it had sung all night.

I spent ten minutes poring though my new set of little family photos in my less-than-a-year-old wallet. Then, staring with unfocussed morning eyes at the top of the tent, I thought in turn about each of my three children, now living far away. We've had so many good times. Throughout their lives, Jill and I went family-camping with them at every opportunity, in countless great places. I'm so proud of them all. Besides our experiences as a group of five, I've been fortunate to share special one-to-one paddling times with each of my kids. As I lounged in the tent on that last morning beside the water, I dreamed we might somehow be able to do a few of those sorts of things again somewhere, someday, sometime.

Telepathically I wished my son Patrick a happy nineteenth birthday, and hoped I would arrive back in the city in time to phone him in Vancouver. I thought of three other memorable July 13ths, such as five years earlier, when the two of us were paddling alone in the old Mad River for a week on the beautiful north shore of Lake Superior, west of Michipicoten. We decided to stop and camp at a glorious place we dubbed "Pat's Beach." Then for three days we enjoyed being the only people for several kilometres along that wonderful wilderness coast. Years earlier, I had brought him and some of his young buddies on a paddle-in birthday camping trip, using our two canoes. After a splash-fight between the boats near the shore, his birthday cake, with candles, had been pancakes cooked over the fire. Of course, I also remembered wrapping my canoe on the Mountain River back on his fourth birthday!

My older son Daniel also paddled with me on numerous river and lake trips in our old Mad River, including four on Lake Superior, a couple of which were especially treasured times with just the two of us. Always one to love camping, adventure and nature, some of Dan's earliest expressions of artistic abilities were done in sketchbooks on trips. When very young he liked copying Haida drawings, sometimes using a magnifying glass to burn them into souvenir pieces of driftwood. Along with his many other skills and talents, Dan had recently become a very successful specialist in computer-generated visual effects in Vancouver. I wondered whether, with his professional abilities, he might perhaps be able to do a realistic rendering that would do justice to that wonderful surprise burst of little white butterflies.

Dan had been in my bow on that earlier Petawawa River trip when I returned the piece of moose spine to the river. I smiled, thinking of the scene again, and also remembered the simple shiny quarter I had tossed into the water back at the start of the Big Thompson portage this time around. I had given such a small token to the river, and marvelled at how much the river had given to me. On the last leg of that long-ago trip with Dan, the four of us had lashed our two canoes together, used two big branches from the shore as masts, and rigged our large tarp as a sail. The wind had blown us along like a speedboat, all the way down this McManus Lake, to the beach that I lay beside. That time, Jill was there waiting for us, smiling away.

My daughter Jody, the oldest of our Three Amigos, has been a water baby from birth. Now a marine biologist, she had just returned to Canada for a visit, after studying dolphins in New Zealand for two years. I thought of a very early precious memory, when she was a small baby, wrapped up in a blanket like a little bundle, and stuffed in front of Jill in the nose of the bow of some rental canoe. This was before we owned our first boat. In my mind's eye, I clearly saw her little eyes smiling back at Jill and I, full of wonder at everything she saw, as our young family paddled along a quiet lake somewhere.

As she grew, Jody and I paddled many lakes and rivers together, including whitewater, first in the old Fiberglass, then in the Mad River. In the Florida Everglades, on one of our camping-Christmas holidays when she was a girl, we paddled a rental canoe with young Dan sitting on the floor in the middle, and got perhaps just a little too close to a crocodile.

But we retreated without incident. On a March Break holiday when she was a teenager, we even did a trip together in our old Mad River on a blackwater river in South Carolina, lined with tall bald-cypress trees draped with long beards of Spanish moss. Those living pillars stood like sentries in the water as we silently paddled through them.

Now grown, and skilled on all kinds of water, Jody is out there on a research boat on the vast ocean almost every day, working to protect sea creatures and plants, and the water itself. I had recently tried to gently talk her into coming back to Ontario, where I pointed out she could use her excellent marine biologist skills to work on the many needy causes closer to home. She had simply smiled at me with understanding and explained, "I like my water with salt."

It was so nice to have a little free-floating time to think about family memories for a bit, but now it was time to stop lolling about, and get going! I crawled out of the tent, had another skinny dip, and got dressed. After making and eating a quick breakfast, I drank my three cups of coffee while packing up. Although I had used my little stove to cook and hadn't lit a fire during my brief stay, out of habit I collected some dry firewood. Whatever the weather might be, or the time of day or night when the next camper might arrive, they would find enough wood for a fire waiting. Of course, I also no-traced-the-place, and packed out a few small human-made items that had been there when I came. Maybe that's part of the reason I couldn't just leave my old boat in the forest or the river. It would have been disrespectful littering.

In half an hour everything was packed and sitting beside the car. From the trunk, I emptied all ropes, bungee cords, canoe sponges, and anything else that might possibly be used to help secure the wrecked boat, and put them into the body of the car. My gear went in the trunk. The new canoe was gently placed on top of the Corolla, resting on four sponges, bow-forwards, as is my custom. I worried about the roof perhaps giving in under the combined weight of the two boats, and wished I had my metal roof racks. But they were at home on Jill's car. I tied the boat down, and did my final sweep.

If the park people allowed me to drive down the hydro corridor track and retrieve the wreck, my plan was to remove all the strings, ropes and branches I had put into it, in my attempt to brace the hull for its journey on the river. Hopefully the hollow shell would then be able to slip right over top of the hull of the new boat. Both of them would be held off of the roof by only the sponges under the new canoe. Once they were nestled snugly together, I would secure them firmly with ropes, and drive home.

When the car was ready, I walked down to the beautiful sand and gravel beach one last time, and took a good look around. I rinsed my hands and face. It was 8:00: time to go. I filtered a final full litre bottle of water, had a long drink, burned some sweetgrass, and said Meegwetch once more. After taking my last look upstream, to the places gone by, I walked back to the parking area, started the car, and headed for Achray.

As always after camping, being in the car felt so lovely. What incredible comfort machines! I deeply appreciated the softness of the seats, the fresh breeze blowing in the windows, and the wonder that came from zooming through the natural world at a pace faster than I had in several days. How the Voyageurs would have loved this method of portaging their canoes and cargo! My camp-coffee had also kicked in. With impeccable timing, I had just finished the very last grounds. Everything felt fabulous, and indeed, it truly was wonderful on this beautiful morning. I couldn't wait to see Jill's face.

The car rolled quietly into the sleepy Achray campground, and stopped in front of the staff building around 8:30. My timid first knocks at the dorm got no answer, so I left the car in the campground parking lot, and wandered around. The sign in the window of the little store, located in the old stone building beside Grand Lake, said it didn't open until 9:00. So I just walked a little more, feeling really good. I also enjoyed the luxuries of the campground facilities, including the toilets and running water in the washroom.

A small old log house, close to the stone building, was the park building where Tom Thomson had worked for a summer. It's now a small museum and art gallery. Fortunately, it was open and empty. My appreciation of art is always sharpened whenever I've spent extended time in the natural world, so I took my time touring it, savouring the beautiful prints of paintings and the history panels. Back outside, it was already getting hot, so for a little while I lay down and just lounged on the wide, flat wooden bench on the shaded porch.

After walking some more, and chatting with a staff member who came along in a park pickup truck, I tried knocking at the dorm door again, a little louder. This time I got an answer. I asked the woman who opened the door if she, or someone there, knew if the service road underneath the hydro corridor had a locked gate, because I wanted to go down there to get something that I had left by the river. She asked me what it was. When I answered "a boat" she turned back inside and called out a more senior warden.

I gave him a condensed version of my story, and told him I would really appreciate being allowed to go down the service road. Part way through, two other men came out. They had overheard my words from inside, and were curious to see me again. Here before me stood the same two wardens that had checked our permits and chatted with Jill and I back at Lake Travers!

They couldn't believe I had actually found my old boat – and even retrieved it! We laughed, and I went over the story again. Through the magic of my little digital camera they were also able to clearly see some of the action. Eyes popped and eyebrows were raised, especially when they saw the pictures that were taken by the woman in the mango canoe of me doing the canoe-over-canoe manoeuvre with the old boat, and also the photos Lindsay had taken of me standing beside my two red canoes holding the "Mad" sign. The camera was passed around twice, and I think the undeniable digital proof quickly transformed their opinion of me, from being just a fool, into being a fool they respected.

As the almost magical coincidences of this trip continued, the senior warden then told me that park regulations would not allow me to go down that service road. He also said it was rare that any park staff ever went down it. However, to my amazement, he said they were going to be going down there that day! – in just half an hour!

He and another warden would be leaving soon with a driver in a pickup, to be dropped off with a canoe at the exact location beside the bridge where I had left my old boat! From there, they would paddle down the rest of the canoe route to McManus, checking campsites along the way. After dropping off the men, the driver would be able to pick up my old boat, and bring it back to me at Achray. He said the truck should be back in a couple of hours. This was fantastic news! I tried to get them to let me go with them, but it couldn't be allowed. So off they went while I waited.

I walked around some more and discovered the little store was now open – and it sold ice cream! I had a second-breakfast binge of two ice cream bars, a mini bag of chips, and a cold drink. Ah, Civilization! After nine days in the wild it was just the thing. I relaxed by the dock and watched as two groups of trippers came in, and two others departed. The total of five cars involved, seemed like such a huge amount of traffic. Then I went back and lay down for another hour on the bench on Tom's front porch.

Letting my mind wander again, I thought of Thomson and his painting friends, and imagined what the park would have looked like to their eyes. Almost everything would have been recently heavily logged, or burned, and the surrounding hills would be just beginning to re-grow their pine, cedar, hemlock, birch and maple. There would also be jack pine, one of which Tom Thomson made forever famous. I marvelled to think of the large number of beautiful paintings he had created in just the last few years before he died. Some of them had been painted there at Achray or nearby. And one at least, I'm convinced, had been painted while he was in the Stone Throne.

My calculations predicted the driver should be back sometime after 11:00, so around 11:15 I wandered over to the parking area. At the exact moment that I started walking away from my car, the pickup drove into the parking lot, and pulled up beside me. I stood with my new canoe on one side, resting securely on its four sponges on the roof of my Corolla, while parallel to it, on my other side, sitting on top of the metal full-frame truck racks, was my old boat. Lost no more.

The driver and I chatted briefly, then he drove over to the small shady parking area by the dorm building. I pulled my car up too. After a few initial questions about how I planned to transport this beat-up thing on my car, we hauled it off the truck, and lay it down, right-side up on the ground. As it came off, I was reminded how fragile it was. I went to work, stripping it of the rough frame of branches, ropes and duct tape. The driver was quite helpful, and used his screwdriver to ease off the few remaining gunwale screws a bit, so their sharp tips wouldn't scratch the hull of the new boat.

In less than an hour we had hoisted the old canoe up onto my car and slipped it gently right over top of the upside-down new one. I was relieved to see the roof didn't sag much. The added weight was probably only about eighteen kilograms (forty pounds). The body of the empty hull spread open easily, wide enough to slide snugly over the bottom of the new boat. The old stern perched just above the new bow, but was forced to bend upwards by major rips in the Royalex. The scene gave the impression of a dead skin in the process of being shed from a sleek new living body. Despite everything, those two canoes looked pretty darn good together.

After securing both canoes with about eight ropes, I was ready to roll. The driver took a few pictures of the finished rig for me, using my camera, then a couple with one of his own, to show his buddies. The two wardens that he dropped off had asked him to do this, to show them how this rigging, using only sponges for support, would work.

With thanks and a big wave, I rolled away. My new boat was still good as new, my lost old boat had been found, and we were all going home.

The tie-down job proved stable. After a careful start, and a couple of stops in the park to adjust for shifting, I became satisfied that the rig should be able make the mechanized portage safely. I expected occasional gusts of winds from passing transport trucks might give the whole thing some big jiggles once on the highway, but the boats should stay firmly on. I would stop as many times as necessary, to ensure everything stayed safe.

I thought to myself, how much better it was to have this kind of trophy on top of my vehicle than any dead animal that might give a hunter some kind of pride. Mine was a very personal satisfaction and happiness, the kind that comes with resolution and closure, with triumph over hopelessness. Boy did I feel good! I grinned at everyone along the way who stared up at my strange rig.

Half way back, I phoned Roger, my good friend and a paddling buddy since our Mountain River days. He knew what had happened to my old boat. When I told him briefly what I had on top of my car that day, he took some time out of his busy work day as I came into town, to meet me briefly in a parking lot for a look. Last fall after my ordeal, he had said to me, with sincere poignancy, "How could you just leave her there? We've been through some rough times with boats Phil, but we've never left one." He understood the depth of my loss.

After his initial bug-eyed walk around my car, Roger laughed and said, "We'll get her floating again! Maybe not for whitewater, but we'll get her on the water, you wait and see." What a great friend. "Who knows," I thought. "Maybe?"

At 5:00 pm, on Patrick's nineteenth birthday, and the fifteenth anniversary of my Mountain River canoe wipe-out, I drove into my driveway with both boats on top of the car. Jill was out somewhere, so I parked on an angle in the driveway, to take a few end-of-the-trip photos. Just as I stood back to take the first picture, she drove up, the kayak still on the roof racks. Her face was wonderful! She stopped and got out, astonished. She fully understood the significance of what she was seeing. Part Two of our special trip was done, my solo was finished, and I was home safe with much more than my intended mission accomplished.

Several pictures later, I wheeled the car under our double carport, and Jill pulled in beside me. Exhausted but very happy, I went in the house and started telling her my new story. Too tired to even empty the car of its contents that evening, the two of us just talked, laughed, hugged, ate, and relaxed. I phoned Patrick, then went to sleep early, on our wonderful, big, soft bed.

In the morning, after more pictures, I untied the old hull and slid her gently off of the new one. With my head inside the middle, I carried it, using a modified solo-portage style. Because it had so many cuts and tears, and no yoke, it bent down over me like a 90-degree hinge. The ends flopped and bounced with each step, all the way around to the back yard. Such a sorry sight. But at least she was home. I set her to rest on the old ping pong table that was there. It hadn't been used since the last of our kids moved away.

I lifted Jill's kayak off her car, and put it on its sawhorses a few metres from the ping pong table. My new canoe was also returned to the back yard, to rest on its own saw horses, near the cedar hedge, by the shed, beside the old Fiberglass. The whole fleet was back to port.

I unloaded, unpacked, and started doing laundry.

Afterword

My broken old canoe sat on that ping pong table in our back yard quite a long time. Over weeks and months, a few friends came by, were told the details of my story, shown some photos, then brought around back for a viewing. I usually left it upside down to keep the rain out, but when a visitor came, we would each take an end and gently roll it over, so we could look at it upright. The vision of that gutted old hull with no seats, yoke, or thwarts, no gunwales except a couple of short splintered sticks, and its many cuts, scars and areas of deformed plastic, did more explaining than any words I could say. Most people just shook their heads in wonder. Some did so in sadness, especially friends who had known her over the years. It was a pitiful, sobering site, like a crashed car.

And me? I was just glad she was there, not missing out in the darkness somewhere. My lost boat had made it home. I would proudly show people my souvenir sign, the red piece of ABS plastic with the word Mad on it in white decal letters, that had come off into my hands as I raised her out of the river by the big cliffs.

Now and then, going about my daily living, I would think about the old boat, and wander into the back yard alone. Sometimes I would just stand and look. There were a lot of feelings.

Almost everyone asked me what I would do with it. For a long time, I said I didn't know, that for the time being I just wanted it to be there, resting in my yard. Sometimes I would wonder if maybe, with a lot of time, money, and work, perhaps using wire stitching, lots of Kevlar and epoxy, replacement gunwales, new thwarts, new seats... maybe she could float again. But there was no way.

Occasionally I let myself ponder how on earth it might have travelled there, all the way to the Big Cliffs site, two full kilometres downriver from Rollway. It seems magical, even mystical, that it went to the precise place we had been heading for when the wreck happened. Surely there was a part of the story that I didn't know. Other people may have seen it in the river somewhere along its way. Probably at least someone had. Maybe things like the blue sponges, a seat, or a couple of bolts, might have been salvaged by other trippers.

I don't need to know. It doesn't matter. If somehow that boat, or any part of it, assisted anyone on their way, I'm glad. Maybe it might have helped some other travellers tell a good story or two around their campfires. I'm just happy she was there when I arrived.

Late the following summer, a year after bringing the broken hull home, and two full years after my wreck, I was out doing a major clean-up of my yard. It was long overdue. Two aspen trees had cracked and were bent over, about to fall. They were rotten, with a million ants inside. Using my chainsaw, I spent two full days cutting them up. Because the wood was so full of bugs, it wasn't usable as firewood. There was also a large pile of old decomposing thin logs in our yard, left over from the damage of a major ice storm many years back. Plus our basement was cluttered with some useless junk. It was time to rent a large truck, load it all in, and haul everything to the dump.

Once the big box truck was in the driveway and most of the rotten wood and junk loaded inside, I took a long break. Walking slowly around my beautiful yard, I thought some very hard thoughts. I knew I had to make my decision, the difficult one I'd been avoiding.

There was no way that my ruined old canoe could ever float again. I had known that back at those Petawawa cliffs, before I even started trying to patch it and bring it home. It was very good for me to have found it and brought it back, to have had it around, and to know that at least she wasn't lost out there anymore. It had been a long goodbye. But I'd always known that someday, I would have to take the last step, and let go permanently.

Looking at how nice my newly cleaned-up yard looked, I felt full acceptance finally settle inside. The decision became obvious and clear. It was time. And it was OK. I went and got my gloves, goggles, and the chainsaw.

With plastic chips flying, the powerful saw sliced easily down into the ABS. I set aside a couple of pieces to keep: the remaining stern deck with its broken sticks of still-attached gunwales, a metre-long section of the ABS side, from the point where the sign had broken off, and of course the Mad sign itself. Who knows, they might be put back into service someday, perhaps even as material for spare parts for my new boat. In less than ten minutes, what was left of my old canoe was cut into four big chunks that fit easily into the back of the rental truck. I took the old ping pong table apart and threw it in as well.

The truck was full to the roof when I drove it to the land-fill. Heaving everything off at the dump, I said one last quick goodbye. I told myself it wasn't my boat anymore, just pieces of old plastic. I left it all, and drove away.

When I got home, I carried my new canoe down the street to the river, and went for a solo paddle.

At the End of the Portage

At the end of this portage
My ready boat waits
To float me through the next
Of this river's gates

The trail's been up and down,
With its slips and its falls
Splendour and drudgery,
Wind and birds' calls

And that last look upstream
To the places gone by
And the river, the river,
Always running by and nigh…

The run looks so tempting,
So crazy, so wild
I look at it old man,
And young man, and child

And who knows exactly
What's waiting for me
Around the next corner,
Think I'll go and see.

As the sun won't last too long,
Clouds always bring rain
I wonder if ever
I'll be back here again…

So I'd best look around,
Soak it up while I can
Changes will come,
Rivers run, rivers ran.

At the end of this portage
My ready boat waits.

Phil Weir, Dumoine River, July 1997

About the Author

Phil Weir was born in downtown Toronto in 1951. Thanks to his family, groups like the Boy Scouts, and summer camps, he escaped the city on treasured trips into the wild, and developed an enduring love of nature and canoeing. He graduated from the University of Toronto in 1972, where he met and married Jill McNamee. In 1973 Phil and Jill moved to Ottawa and both eventually became teachers.

They had three wonderful children, and the family did scores of wonderful camping trips together. As a high school teacher Phil always found ways to include Outdoor Education. This was done via field trips, clubs, leading and promoting an Outdoor Ed. credit course, curriculum development, and also full-time teaching for five years at the MacSkimming Outdoor Education Centre. Now retired from paid teaching, Phil still enjoys encouraging people to know, to understand, and to love the natural world, and their place in it. In 2013 he created Wildwaters Publishing.

Published in Canada by : Wildwaters Publishing.
For information on how to purchase either
End of the Portage: A Canoe Memoir or
Canoeing the Mountain: Gifts from the Waters

please see: **www.wildwaterspublishing.com**

WILDWATERS

CPSIA information can be obtained
at www.ICGtesting.com
Printed in the USA
LVOW12s0714240817
546160LV00003BA/3/P